PENNSYLVANIA
PATRIOTS

Their Lives, Contributions,
and Burial Sites

JOE FARRELL • LAWRENCE KNORR • JOE FARLEY

SUNBURY
PRESS
Mechanicsburg, PA USA

Published by Sunbury Press, Inc.
Mechanicsburg, Pennsylvania

SUNBURY
P R E S S
www.sunburypress.com

For information about special discounts for bulk purchases, please contact Sunbury Press Orders Dept. at (855) 338-8359 or orders@sunburypress.com.

To request one of our authors for speaking engagements or book signings, please contact Sunbury Press Publicity Dept. at publicity@sunburypress.com.

ISBN: 978-1-62006-106-0 (Trade paperback)

Library of Congress Control Number: 2019953371

FIRST SUNBURY PRESS EDITION: October 2019

Product of the United States of America
0 1 1 2 3 5 8 13 21 34 55

Set in Adobe Garamond
Designed by Crystal Devine
Cover by Lawrence Knorr
Edited by the authors

Continue the Enlightenment!

Contents

Foreword

———•◦•———

Pennsylvania, where the Declaration of Independence and the United States Constitution were adopted, was essential to the birth of the nation. It not only hosted the conventions that produced the most important governance documents since the Magna Carta, but it also provided men and women of courage who helped breathe life into the new republic.

Those founding fathers and mothers bequeathed our nation to us through great sacrifice. Of the fifty-six signers of the Declaration of Independence, five were captured by the British as traitors and tortured before they died. Twelve had their homes burned to the ground. While some of the details have been clouded by time, they, pledged their lives, their fortunes, and their sacred honor to that cause.

In this important study of *Pennsylvania Patriots*, Joe Farrell, Joe Farley, and Lawrence Knorr pay tribute to some of the people who guided our country through its most severe challenges. The book makes it clear that Pennsylvanians have earned their rightful place in our nation's history. It highlights citizens who spent most of their lives in the service of our Commonwealth and our country and, in fact, chose Pennsylvania as their final resting places.

While everybody knows about the wit and wisdom of Benjamin Franklin or the utopian idealism of William Penn, other patriots deserve similar recognition.

John Dickinson, for example, provided a thoughtful, practical voice to the deliberations of the Continental Congress. Amid a growing call to arms, he reminded his colleagues about the mortal danger of war with the mightiest power on earth. He was castigated for being the only delegate to abstain from signing the Declaration but was correct in his assessment of the crucible that the colonies were about to face. That did not deter him from taking command of a militia battalion and fighting alongside his colleagues for the cause.

He also stood out among his peers when he warned of the cancer of slavery and fought to address the issue when the Constitution was being drafted. In the end, his thoughtfulness and vision earned him the highest praise from a former adversary. John Dickinson, said John Adams, was "first among equals."

Pennsylvania Patriots also features a woman of great courage. Mary Hays McCauley was reported to have cared for American soldiers at the decisive Battle of Monmouth. She had accompanied her husband to the fight and braved artillery fire to bring water and supplies to the men. When her husband was critically wounded, she took up his arms and fought on. She is revered in Pennsylvania and throughout the nation as Molly Pitcher. Her resting place is Carlisle, Pennsylvania.

Another of my favorites is Dr. Benjamin Rush. Wealthy conservatives and timid moderates supported the established order of King George III and dominated The Pennsylvania General Assembly. That body instructed its delegates to the Continental Congress to vote *against* independence. Enter Dr. Benjamin Rush, who led the shopkeepers, the craftsmen, and the middle-class in opposition to their state government. These "radicals" took their fervor down the street to Carpenters' Hall where the Continental Congress was meeting. There, they adopted a preliminary version of the Declaration and gave Thomas Jefferson an outline for his famous essay. The "radicals" also "went public" at a protest rally at the doorstep of the General Assembly. Four thousand Philadelphians joined them to demand nothing less than a new state government with the courage to act.

Pennsylvania Patriots also highlights a relatively unknown whose writings continue to resonate at all levels of government today. Few people know that Tench Coxe descended from leaders who advocated for uniting the American colonies as early as 1722. He gave up a thriving merchant business that catered to the British army to join the revolutionary cause. He made it his responsibility to take on British leaders when they disarmed the citizens of Philadelphia and was the first to insist that they have a "right to keep and bear their private arms."

And let's not forget "Mad" Anthony Wayne. A surveyor and a tanner, Wayne served one year in the Provincial Assembly before he headed off to war. He commanded forces at Brandywine, Paoli, and Germantown in Pennsylvania and won some strategic victories in Virginia. History paints Anthony Wayne as a firebrand who rode brashly into the teeth of battle. It was his compassion; not his "madness" that got him through the bitter winter at Valley Forge with Commander George Washington and their troops.

Pennsylvania and the nation owe their existence to the patriots who were willing to take on the existing power structure in legislative halls and on the battlefield. Through six bloody years of war and in the crucial formative years that followed, these are the people who made it possible for Pennsylvanians to live and prosper in the Commonwealth that we enjoy today.

When Benjamin Franklin was leaving the Constitutional Convention in Philadelphia, a citizen approached him and asked: "Dr. Franklin, what have you given us?" Franklin's reply was simple and profound: "A republic, if you can keep it."

Pennsylvania Patriots reminds us that we owe our predecessors more than respect. We owe them a recommitment of our own lives and fortunes to the experiment for which they fought and died. This book helps all of us to remember our roles in "keeping" the Commonwealth and the republic.

Mark Singel
Former Lieutenant Governor of Pennsylvania

Introduction

As a student of history, and both a former Mayor of the city of Philadelphia and Governor of the Keystone State, I support all efforts to bring to light the contributions of the remarkable men and women who worked tirelessly and with tremendous risk to aid in the effort to establish this great nation. I note, with a considerable amount of pride, much of the work resulting in the founding of the United States of America took place in Pennsylvania. Many Pennsylvanians were instrumental and invaluable in the effort. This volume both educates and reminds the reader of the people who were at the forefront of a revolution that turned the world upside down. It reflects parts of our history that should be welcomed and savored as our country approaches its 250th birthday. This book tells the amazing story of our nation's birth, the difficulties our founders faced, and the ultimate triumph of freedom. This was even more remarkable when you consider that our founders were the most successful people in the colonies—"we pledge to each other our lives, our **fortunes** and our sacred honor"—and still risked everything for the cause of freedom and liberty. Given the above, it brings me great pleasure to introduce this book, *Pennsylvania Patriots*.

I first met the authors in the spring of 2018 when we sat together in my Philadelphia office to discuss their project to write a multiple-volume series on the nation's founders. They also brought to my attention the distressing fact that the gravesites of some of the nation's original heroes had been neglected, and in some cases rendered inaccessible. They shared pictures of overgrown, weedy, disheveled graves marked by broken monuments. They said they hoped bringing these conditions to the public's attention would result in efforts to restore some sites, relocate others, and create new historical markers to remember better the contributions made by these distinguished Americans. This book is more than an excellent guide to educate Americans on the beginnings of their storied history; it is also a call for action. I heartily endorse those efforts and commend Joe Farrell, Joe Farley, and Lawrence Knorr for taking on this task.

The book itself represents an excellent starting point to begin a study of Pennsylvania's vital contributions to the establishment of our republic. The short biographical sketches are designed to whet the reader's appetite and create a desire to learn more about the men and women who fill these pages. Naturally, the Commonwealth's most famous are covered. The lives of Benjamin Franklin, James Wilson, Robert Morris, Benjamin Rush, Molly Pitcher, and Betsy Ross are told in a concise manner that still holds surprises for the reader to discover. The lives of lesser-known but just as indispensable supporters of the Patriot cause are given their just due. There is the story of General "Mad Anthony" Wayne who was one of Washington's favorite generals because of his willingness to take on the British forces. This account includes details on how his remains came to be buried in two places in Pennsylvania hundreds of miles apart. The interesting tale of Commodore John Barry tells of the man who came to be called by contemporaries "the Father of the American Navy." One will also find details on the life of Haym Solomon, a Jewish immigrant from Poland who lost two fortunes supporting the cause of independence and then died bankrupt. These are but a few of the many interesting characters explored in this volume.

The authors have drawn on their rich experience in compiling these stories in the concise but informative manner they have mastered. The trio have utilized the style that has worked so effectively in their eleven-volume series *Keystone Tombstones* which chronicles the lives of many of the famous individuals who were laid to rest in Pennsylvania. *The Pittsburgh Post Gazette* reported the pleasures of the series comes with "The 'I can't believe I didn't know that' moments which are everywhere." *Pennsylvania Patriots* is sure to provide similar delights to the reader.

The authors have found a way to bring to life the people involved and tell of the important events in which they played vital parts. The stories chronicle the beginning of American resistance to British rule leading to the successful Revolution and the formative events that followed. The subsequent Constitutional Convention is covered as are the difficulties faced by those who established the first government under the document adopted by those renowned men who came together in 1787 in Pennsylvania. Thus, the story of the nation's founding is brought into the light by an examination of the lives of those who contributed every step along the often dangerous and contentious way. As we approach the United States Semiquincentennial anniversary, this is a book that can bring all Americans together in the true spirit of celebration.

The lives and events covered within these pages impacted humanity around the world as much if not more than any great scientific discovery. As the former Governor of the state that served as the focal point of many of the events resulting in the creation of the United States of America, I wholeheartedly applaud the publication of this work. Without reservation, I recommend it to anyone who wants to learn more about this nation's founding and the men and women who risked all to make it possible.

Edward G. Rendell
Former Governor of Pennsylvania
Former Mayor of Philadelphia

Benjamin Franklin
(1706–1790)

The First American

Buried at Christ Church Burial Grounds,
Philadelphia, Pennsylvania.

Declaration of Independence • U.S. Constitution • Diplomat

Referred to as "The First American" by historian H. W. Brands and others, it is not exaggerating to say that no Pennsylvanian is as well known or as well respected as Benjamin Franklin. He excelled at so many things. He was an author, a political theorist, a scientist, an inventor, a diplomat and politician (though he might disagree), and a revolutionary. He was well into middle age when he began to agitate for the colonies and became the senior statesman throughout the American Revolution, involved in the formulation of the new nation's key documents and treaties.

Benjamin's father, Josiah Franklin, was born in the village of Ecton, Northamptonshire, England where he married his first wife, Anne Child, in 1677. The couple arrived in America in 1683. By that time, they had three children, and after arriving in America, they had four more. Josiah made a living as a printer and candle-maker. After his first wife died, he married Abiah Folger, the daughter of a miller, and had ten more children. Benjamin Franklin was born in Boston, Massachusetts on January 17, 1706. He was Josiah's 15th child and his last son.

Franklin's parents wanted a career in the church for him. He was sent to the Boston Latin School, but after two years, his parents could

Benjamin Franklin

no longer make the payments to allow him to continue. Franklin never graduated, but through his reading, he continued what would be called a self-education. At the age of twelve, he went to work for his brother James, a printer, who taught him the trade. James founded *The New England Courant*, the first independent newspaper in the colonies. Franklin began to write letters to the paper under the name of Mrs. Silence Dogood. The views expressed became the subject of conversation around Boston. When James discovered that Franklin was the famous author, he punished him. In addition to verbal abuse, his brother was known to beat Franklin. Having had enough, Franklin fled his apprenticeship at age seventeen, and according to the laws of the time, became a fugitive.

Franklin arrived in Philadelphia in 1723, seeking a fresh start. With his experience, he was able to find work in printing shops. Pennsylvania's

Royal Governor William Keith convinced Franklin to return to England
to find the equipment needed to start
a new newspaper in Philadelphia.
When the governor failed to provide the backing for the enterprise,
Franklin found work in a printer's
shop in London. He returned to
Philadelphia in 1726 and went to
work for a merchant as a clerk, shop-
keeper, and a bookkeeper.

Franklin organized a group of
men known as the Junto in 1727.
The goal of the group was to engage
in activities that would improve the

The first stamp of the United States
featured Ben

members as individuals and at the same time, benefit the community.
The group created a library. Franklin came up with the idea to form
a subscription library to increase the number of books available. The
members combined their funds to buy additional books that would be
available for all to read. Franklin hired the first librarian in 1732.

In 1728, Franklin's employer passed away, and Franklin returned to
the printing business. The next year, he became the publisher of a newspaper called *The Pennsylvania Gazette*. The newspaper provided Franklin
with a mechanism to make known his views on the important issues of
the time. His observations were well received, and his stature continued
to grow. Wrote Franklin in his autobiography, "I took care not only to
be in reality industrious and frugal but to avoid all appearance to the
contrary. I dressed plainly; I was seen at no place of idle diversions. I
never went out fishing or shooting . . ."

In 1730, Franklin entered into what would be called a common-law
marriage with Deborah Reed. He could not marry Reed because she already had a husband, though he had abandoned her. One of the reasons
that may have led Franklin to make this decision was the fact that he had
recently acknowledged that he was the father of an illegitimate son named
William, and he wanted to provide his son a family life. William's mother
remains unknown. Benjamin and Deborah had two other children. The

first was a son named Francis, who was born in 1732 and died in 1736. The second child, a daughter named Sarah, was born in 1743.

During this period, Franklin also began a career as an author. In 1733, he began to publish *Poor Richard's Almanac*. Franklin seldom published under his name, and in this instance, the author was identified as Richard Saunders. Some of his witty adages such as "Fish and visitors stink in three days" are still quoted today. Though published under the name Saunders, it was common knowledge that Franklin was the author. His reputation continued to grow. The almanac itself was a tremendous success, selling about 10,000 copies per year. In today's world, that would translate to nearly three million copies.

Franklin founded the American Philosophical Society in 1743. The purpose of this organization was to provide a forum where scientific men, like himself, could discuss their projects and discoveries. It was around this time that Franklin began studying electricity. That study would remain a part of his life until the day he died. The story of the kite, the string, and the key is probably a false one. The television show *MythBusters* simulated the supposed experiment and concluded that if Franklin had proceeded as described, it would have killed him.

In addition to his scientific studies, Franklin was also an inventor. Among his more noted inventions are the Franklin stove, the lightning rod, and bifocal lenses. Franklin viewed his devices as yet another way he could help improve society.

In 1747, Franklin decided to get out of the printing business. He formed a partnership whereby David Hall would run the company, and the two would share the profits. This provided Franklin with a steady income and also gave him the time to pursue his studies and other interests. His writings, inventions, and discoveries had by now made him well known throughout the colonies and in Europe.

As he grew older, Franklin became more and more interested in public affairs. He was drawn into Philadelphia politics and was soon elected to the post of councilman. In 1749 he became a Justice of the Peace, and two years later, he was elected to the Pennsylvania Assembly.

In 1753, he was appointed to the post of joint deputy postmaster general of North America. In this role, he worked to reform the postal

Poor Richard's Almanac

system. Among his accomplishments was the adoption of the practice to deliver mail weekly. During this time, Franklin founded the first hospital in the colonies. Honors continued to come his way. Both Harvard and Yale awarded him honorary degrees.

In September 1753, Franklin was one of the emissaries from Pennsylvania accompanying Conrad Weiser, the Indian agent and interpreter, to Carlisle to negotiate a peace treaty with the Six Nations. Franklin wrote about the influence of rum on the proceedings:

> "We strictly forbade the selling any liquor to them; and, when they complained of this restriction, we told them, that, if they

could continue sober during the treaty, we would give them plenty of rum when the business was over. They claimed and received the rum. In the evening, hearing a great noise among them, the commissioners walked to see what was the matter. We found they had made a great bonfire in the middle of the square; they were all drunk, men and women, quarreling and fighting. Their dark-colored bodies, half-naked, seen only by the gloomy light of the bonfire, running after and beating one another with firebrands, accompanied by their horrid yellings, formed a scene the most resembling our ideas of hell that could well be imagined; there was no appeasing the tumult, and we retired to our lodging. At midnight a number of them came thundering at our door, demanding more rum, of which we took no notice. The next day, sensible that they had misbehaved in giving us that disturbance, they sent three of their old counselors to make their apology. The orator acknowledged the fault, but laid it upon the rum; and then endeavored to excuse the rum by saying, 'The Great Spirit, who made all things, made everything for some use, and whatever use he designed anything for, that use it should be always be put to'; now, when he made rum, he said, 'Let this be for the Indians to get drunk with; and it must be so.' And indeed, if it be the design of Providence to extirpate these savages, in order to make room for the cultivators of the earth, it seems not impossible that rum may be the appointed means. It has already annihilated all the tribes who formerly inhabited the seacoast."

The following May, Franklin was with Weiser again at the Albany Conference to once again treat with the Native Americans. This led to the Albany Purchase of more land in Pennsylvania for the colony, taking most of the Juniata Valley.

As the French and Indian War broke out, Franklin was involved as a representative from Pennsylvania. He visited with General Braddock before his ill-fated 1755 expedition into western Pennsylvania, offering the British general much-needed provisions.

THE LAST RESTING PLACE OF
BENJAMIN FRANKLIN
1706 — 1790

"VENERATED FOR BENEVOLENCE
ADMIRED FOR TALENTS, ESTEEMED
FOR PATRIOTISM BELOVED FOR
PHILANTHROPY"

WASHINGTON

"THE SAGE WHOM TWO WORLDS
CLAIMED AS THEIR OWN"

MIRABEAU

"HE TORE FROM THE SKIES THE
LIGHTNING AND FROM TYRANTS
THE SCEPTRE"

TURGOT

Plaque at Christ Church Burial Ground
near the grave of Franklin

In 1756, the Pennsylvania Assembly allotted funds to Franklin and Weiser to construct forts on the Pennsylvania frontier, essentially along the Blue Mountain. Franklin handled the forts for Berks County and east. Weiser managed the fortifications from Berks County to the Susquehanna River.

In 1757, the Pennsylvania Assembly selected Franklin to go to England to oppose the political favoritism that was being shown to the Penn family who were descended from Pennsylvania's founder William Penn. The family was exempt from paying any land taxes and retained the right to veto legislation passed by the Pennsylvania Assembly. Franklin worked on this mission for five years, but it failed as the Royal government refused to turn their backs on the Penns.

During his stay in England, more honors came his way. In 1759, the University of Saint Andrews awarded him an honorary degree. Three years later, Oxford followed suit by awarding Franklin an honorary doctorate for his scientific achievements. It was as a result of this award that he became known as Doctor Franklin. To top it off, he also secured an appointment for his illegitimate son William. The younger Franklin was named Colonial Governor of New Jersey.

When Franklin returned to America, the feud between the Penns and the Assembly was ongoing. Franklin became the leader of the anti-Penn party known as the Anti-proprietary Party. In 1764 he was elected Speaker of the Pennsylvania House. As the speaker, Franklin attempted to change Pennsylvania from proprietary to royal government. The move was not popular with the voting populous who feared that such a change would infringe on their freedoms. As a result, Franklin was defeated in the elections held in October of 1764. After his defeat, the Anti-propriety Party sent him back to England to try yet again to fight the influence of the Penn family.

While in London, Franklin spoke out in opposition to the Stamp Act of 1765, but the measure passed over his objections. This did not deter him, and he continued to fight the Act. His efforts contributed to its eventual repeal. As a result, he became the leading representative of American interests in England.

During his time in Europe, Franklin decided to tour Ireland. This visit would have a profound effect on him. When he witnessed the poverty in Ireland, he became convinced that it was a result of regulations and laws similar to those through which England was governing America. He concluded that America would suffer a fate similar to Ireland's if England's colonial exploitation continued.

Franklin's common-law wife never accompanied him overseas because of her fear of the ocean. While he was on this trip, she implored him to return to America. She claimed she was ill and blamed her condition on his absence. Franklin stayed in England, and Deborah Reed died as a result of a stroke in 1774.

Franklin returned to America in May of 1775. By this time, the American Revolution had already begun with the Battles of Lexington and Concord. Pennsylvania selected him as one of their delegates to the Second Continental Congress.

In July of 1775, the Continental Congress appointed Franklin to the post of United States Postmaster General. He was the country's first postmaster. The appointment made sense based on Franklin's previous postal experience. The postal system that was established then evolved into the United States Postal Service that is still operational today.

While serving in Congress, he was appointed to the Committee of Five chosen to draft the Declaration of Independence. Thomas Jefferson did the bulk of the work on the Declaration, though Franklin did make several minor changes to the draft Jefferson provided to the other members of the committee. As the Declaration was signed, the President of Congress, John Hancock, remarked: "We must all hang together." Franklin replied, "Yes, we must indeed all hang together, or most assuredly, we shall all hang separately." At seventy, Franklin was the oldest to sign the document.

Later in 1776, Franklin was sent to France to represent American interests. He was already well known in that country due to his writings, inventions, and scientific discoveries. Wrote John Adams about Franklin in France, "His reputation was more universal than that of Leibnitz or Newton, Frederick or Voltaire, and his character more beloved and esteemed than any or all of them . . . His name was familiar to government and people . . . to such a degree that there was scarcely a peasant not familiar with it, and who did not consider him as a friend to humankind. When they spoke of him, they seemed to think he was to restore the Golden Age."

His appointment bore fruit. Franklin succeeded in securing a military alliance between the United States and France in 1778. This alliance was of critical importance to the Americans in their struggle against England. Most historians doubt that the American Revolution would have succeeded without the help of France. Franklin also played a crucial role in negotiating the Treaty of Paris in 1783. This treaty ended the American Revolution and established the United States as an independent country.

Franklin returned to the United States in 1785. Only George Washington exceeded his stature as a champion of American

Ben and Deborah Franklin's grave

independence. That same year, he was elected President of Pennsylvania, a post that would be similar to the governor today. Franklin served in this position for just over three years.

In 1787 he was selected to serve as a Pennsylvania delegate at the Constitutional Convention in Philadelphia. For four months, the delegates met and argued over whether the country should establish a strong federal government. On the day the voting on the proposed constitution was to take place, many of the delegates believed it would be voted down. Before the voting, Franklin advised the Convention that he had

Detail of Franklin's grave

a few comments to make. At the time he was too frail to deliver the speech himself, so he had fellow Pennsylvania delegate James Wilson read it for him. In the speech, Franklin spoke of his misgivings about the Constitution. However, in the end, he said, "Thus I consent, sir, to this Constitution. The opinions I have of its errors, I sacrifice to the public good." He went on to say, "On the whole, sir, I cannot help expressing a wish that every member of the convention who may still have objections to it would, with me, on this occasion doubt a little of his own infallibility and make manifest our unanimity." When the vote was taken, it was close to unanimous. Only three of the forty-one delegates refused to sign the document, and all thirteen states eventually ratified it.

His public life at an end, Franklin wrote about his pending mortality, "Death is as necessary to the constitution as sleep; we shall rise refreshed in the morning. The course of nature must soon put a period to my present mode of existence. This I shall submit to with less regret, as having seen, during a long life, a good deal of this world, I feel a growing curiosity to become acquainted with some other; and can cheerfully, with filial confidence, resign my spirit to the conduct of that great and good Parent of mankind, who created it, and who has so graciously protected and preserved me from my birth to the present hour."

Franklin died in his Philadelphia home on April 17, 1790. He was 84 years old. He is the only founding father who signed all four of the documents central to the establishment of the United States: the Declaration of Independence, the Treaty of Paris, the Treaty of Alliance with France, and the United States Constitution. Over 20,000 people attended his funeral. He was laid to rest in the Christ Church Burial Ground in Philadelphia. Across the young nation, the front pages of newspapers were bordered in black. Reporting on the funeral, Philadelphia newspapers wrote, "Near the place of internment in Arch Street, 85 minute guns were discharged in the most regular manner by Captain Sommer's company of the militia regiment of artillery, and the vessels in the port of the various foreign nations, as well as our own, hoisted their colors, in the usual order, on the mournful occasion. In short, every possible mark of respect was paid to the manes of this venerable and illustrious citizen and philosopher." The U.S. House of Representatives declared a month of mourning.

Benjamin Franklin is remembered in too many ways to provide a complete list, but here are a few:

He is the face on the $100 bill, affectionately referred to as a "Benjamin." He has also been on numerous postage stamps.

The following places were named in Franklin's honor:

- The unofficial short-lived State of Franklin. It later became eastern Tennessee.
- Counties in at least sixteen states.
- The Franklin Institute in Philadelphia.
- Franklin and Marshall College in Lancaster.
- Franklin Field in Philadelphia.
- The Benjamin Franklin Bridge across the Delaware River between Philadelphia and Camden, New Jersey.
- Several U.S. Navy ships.

John Armstrong, Sr.
(1717–1795)

The Hero of Kittanning

Buried at Old Graveyard,
Carlisle, Pennsylvania.

———•◦•———

Military • Continental Congress

John Armstrong was a Presbyterian from Northern Ireland who emigrated to Pennsylvania to utilize his surveying skills on behalf of the Penn family. He planned the city of Carlisle and served as a military commander before and during the French and Indian War. When the American Revolution began, he was a brigadier general in the Continental Army and then the Major General of the Pennsylvania Militia. Upon retiring from active duty in 1777, he was elected to the Continental Congress where he continued his advocacy for George Washington and later for the U.S. Constitution.

————◦•◦————

John Armstrong was born on October 13, 1717, in Brookeborough, County Fermanagh, in what is now Northern Ireland. The names of his parents and exact birthplace are lost to history, though there is some belief his father's name was James, and his parents married in 1704. He was one of fifteen children who included Margaret (1737-1817, the wife of Reverend George Duffield (1732-1790); and Rebecca (1738-1828), who was the wife of James Turner (1737-1803).

Armstrong learned surveying and civil engineering in Ireland before emigrating to Delaware and then Pennsylvania in the 1740s. The

John Armstrong, Sr.

exact date of his arrival in Pennsylvania is unknown, but he married Rebecca Lyon Armstrong (1710–1797), the daughter of Archbald and Ann Armstrong, in 1747. According to one biographer, the Armstrongs settled in the Kittatinny (Cumberland) Valley, west of the Susquehanna River. Armstrong worked as a surveyor for the Penns and laid out the first plan for the town of Carlisle, where he was an initial settler.

In 1749, Armstrong got involved in politics and was elected to the Pennsylvania Assembly representing the newly formed York County, which included the new town of Carlisle at that time.

He later surveyed the boundaries of Cumberland County, which was carved out of York County in 1750. In 1751, he was returned to the Pennsylvania Assembly, this time representing the newly formed Cumberland County. He then served in a series of appointed positions, including as a justice of the peace and as a magistrate or judge. In 1754, he was selected as a delegate for Pennsylvania to travel to Albany to negotiate with the colony of Connecticut regarding removing its settlers from the province. There had been a dispute between the colonies regarding borders.

During the French and Indian War, Armstrong served in the British military and used his surveying skills to assist with logistics, cutting trails through the forests for supply routes. He also planned a series of forts in the wilderness of western Pennsylvania.

In 1756, as the commander of Pennsylvania provincial forces, he led British and Pennsylvania troops against the natives in retaliation for the defeat of General Braddock. At Kittanning, a native stronghold along the Allegheny River, Armstrong defeated a large force of Delaware Indians led by chief "Captain Jacobs." Upon the death of the chief in battle, Armstrong's decisive victory led to the rise of Teedyuscung in his place. The new chief, realizing his precarious position, sued for peace. Armstrong, who was injured in the battle and lost seventeen men, became an instant celebrity among the colonials, known as the "Hero of Kittanning."

After the battle, back in Carlisle, Armstrong became a judge in the Court of Common Pleas and was the sole judicial authority for most of the region. He was well-respected for his temperament on the bench.

When General Forbes launched his expedition against Fort Duquesne in 1758, Colonel Armstrong led 2700 Pennsylvania troops. Seeing this large force, the French vacated and destroyed their fort. During this campaign, Armstrong became good friends with a young Virginia militia commander named Colonel George Washington.

In 1763, as part of the campaign against Chief Pontiac, General Armstrong led colonial forces against native Delaware and Monsey towns along the West Branch of the Susquehanna, burning them and destroying their corn.

During the years before the American Revolution, Armstrong continued in service to his community and congregation. In 1773, he was one of the founding trustees of what would become Dickinson College in Carlisle. When its namesake, John Dickinson, could not serve as president, Armstrong served in his place.

At the outbreak of the American Revolution, Armstrong was appointed a brigadier general in the Pennsylvania militia. On March 1, 1776, the Continental Congress gave him the same rank in the Continental Army. George Washington initially sent him to Charleston, South Carolina where he utilized his engineering talents to construct the defenses there. Upon the arrival of General Charles Lee in early April, Armstrong returned to Pennsylvania. There, he was elevated to Major General of the Pennsylvania Militia. Meanwhile, in Charleston, Armstrong's defenses enabled Lee's rebels to withstand the Battle of Sullivan's Island in June 1776.

In charge of Pennsylvania forces, Armstrong saw action following the British invasion of Philadelphia in 1777. At the Battle of Brandywine on September 11, Armstrong's troops held the far left of the American line and guarded the army's supplies. Though the Americans lost, Armstrong was able to escape with the supplies after dark.

The following month, at the Battle of Germantown, Amstrong's forces led the American right, attempting to circumvent the British left to attack their rear. While the attack was going well, there was confusion in the fog leading to a friendly-fire incident between Adam Stephen's men and Anthony Wayne's troops. Despite marching to the center of Germantown, Armstrong's forces had to withdraw.

Following Germantown, with the opposing armies encamped, his health failing, and his old wounds complaining, Armstrong retired from active command at age sixty. He returned home to Carlisle.

On November 20, 1778, Armstrong was elected by the Pennsylvania Assembly to the Continental Congress. He was also re-elected the following year. His tenure of actual service was February 1779 to August 1780.

In a letter to his friend General Horatio Gates, Armstrong complained of the pride and politics of the various representatives who were not focused on the needs of the army. He felt serving in the military was easier. Armstrong also continued a steady correspondence with his friend, George Washington, offering advice and support.

Following his year and a half in Congress, Armstrong returned home to Carlisle and enjoyed a quiet retirement. He participated in numerous civic roles and was an ardent supporter of the new U.S. Constitution. However, it was his son John Jr. who attended the Confederation Congress during its waning months in 1787 and 1788, not him.

The grave of John Armstrong

John and Rebecca Armstrong were the parents of James Armstrong (1748-1828), who married Mary Stevenson (1766-1813), the daughter of George Stevenson, Esquire; and John Armstrong Jr. (1758-1843), who married Alida Livingston (1761-1822), the sister of Robert R. Livingston of the "Committee of Five" and Edward Livingston. John Jr. later became a Continental Congressman, U.S. Senator, and a controversial Secretary of War under President James Madison during the War of 1812.

John Armstrong Sr. died on March 9, 1795, at his home in Carlisle, Pennsylvania. He was laid to rest in the Old Graveyard in Carlisle. His passing was barely noted in the newspapers. One, *The American Minerva* of New York, merely stated, "Died on Monday the 9th instant, Gen. John Armstrong, in an advanced age, being a resident in this town for many years past."

Rebecca Armstrong passed away on November 16, 1797, joining her husband in the Old Cemetery.

In 1800, Pennsylvania created Armstrong County and put its seat at Kittanning.

John Barry
(1745–1803)

The Commodore

Buried at St. Mary's Catholic Churchyard,
Philadelphia, Pennsylvania.

Military

John Barry was an Irish-born naval commander during the American Revolution who after the war became the first commodore in the new United States Navy. Many of his contemporaries dubbed him "The Father of the United States Navy," an epithet he shares with John Paul Jones, Joseph Hewes, and John Adams.

John Barry was born March 25, 1745, in a modest thatched-roof cottage at Ballysampson on Our Lady's Island in Tacumshane parish, County Wexford, Ireland. Barry's father was a tenant farmer who was soon evicted by his British landlord. The family next moved to nearby Rosslare on the coast where Barry's uncle was a fisherman. Young Barry soon found himself a ship's cabin boy thanks to his uncle and progressed from seaman, to able seaman, to a mate.

Barry grew to be six-feet four-inches in height, an imposing figure in those times. He was also intelligent. He learned navigational skills by combining mathematics, astronomy, and meteorology.

Around 1760, at the age of fifteen, he came to Philadelphia to find employment in the growing merchant trade. By twenty-one, he was a

Commodore John Barry

master seaman and earned command of his ship, *Barbados*. Barry developed a reputation as a fair captain who cared about the men working for him. He was also a devout Christian, beginning each morning by reading passages from his Bible.

"Big John" Barry made no less than nine trips to the West Indies without incident. This reliability, along with his personable nature, led to success in the shipping business. He moved up to a brigantine named the *Patty and Polly*, and then to a schooner named the *Industry*. During this time, Barry married Mary Clary (or Cleary) at Old St. Joseph's chapel in Philadelphia on October 24, 1768.

By 1772, Barry's abilities drew the attention of Meredith and Clymer, one of the premier mercantile businesses in Philadelphia. Reese Meredith hired him to command the *Peg*, a much larger vessel. Upon developing a friendship with Robert Morris, the financier, Barry moved to Willing,

Morris, and Cadwalader where he took command of the 200-ton merchant ship *Black Prince*. During this time, Barry set the record (for the 18th century) of traveling 237 miles in 24 hours on a return voyage from England. Unfortunately, while at sea, Barry's wife passed away suddenly at only 29 back in Philadelphia on February 8, 1774. This loss affected Barry greatly.

At the outbreak of the American Revolution, Barry, a patriot from the start, sold his merchant ship *Black Prince* to the cause, outfitting his ship into a warship named *Alfred*, which became the flagship of commander Esek Hopkins. He was assigned to equip other ships for war, overseeing rigging, the piercing of gunports, strengthening of bulwarks, procuring powder and canvas, and loading provisions. Congress recognized this contribution by awarding him a Captain's commission. It was signed by John Hancock, President of Congress, on March 14, 1776, giving him command of his first warship, the brig *Lexington*. Three weeks later, on April 7, 1776, Barry was credited with the first capture of the war, the British sloop *Edward*, caught off the coast of Virginia after a one-hour battle. Barry reported to Congress:

> In sight of the Cape of Virginia
> April 7, 1776
> to the Marine Committee
>
> Gentlemen: I have the pleasure to acquaint you, that at 1:00 P.M. this day, I fell in with the sloop, *Edward* belonging to the *Liverpool* frigate. They killed two of our men and wounded two more. We shattered her in a terrible manner as you will see. I shall give you a particular account of the powder that was taken out of her, as well as my proceedings in general. I have the pleasure to acquaint you that all our people behaved with much courage. This victory had a tremendous psychological effect in boosting American morale, as it was the first capture of a British warship by a regularly commissioned American cruiser.

Barry brought the captured *Edward* into Philadelphia. On June 28, in what became known as the Battle of Turtle Gut Inlet, the brig *Nancy* ran aground while trying to elude the British blockade. Laden with barrels of powder, Barry ordered them rowed ashore during the night, leaving only 100 barrels aboard by dawn. A fuse was lit, and when the British sailors boarded in the morning, the powder exploded. Barry continued to captain the *Lexington* until October 18, 1776, capturing several more vessels during that time.

Next, Barry was given command of the 32-gun *Effingham*, a new frigate under construction in Philadelphia. Tories in Philadelphia offered Barry the tremendous sum of 15,000 guineas in gold or 20,000 pounds sterling plus a commission as a captain in the Royal Navy if he would hand over the *Effingham* to the British when it was ready to sail. Barry emphatically refused "the eyedee of being a treater."

With the *Effingham* under construction, Barry volunteered for the Continental Army. He served with a company of Marines under General John Cadwalader, who had been a part-owner of the shipping company with which he had been affiliated. As Cadwalader's aide-de-camp, Barry participated in the Battles of Trenton and Princeton. Washington chose Barry as a courier to convey the wounded through British lines and to carry a dispatch of a flag of truce to General Cornwallis.

On July 7, 1777, Barry married again, this time taking an attractive and popular Sarah "Sally" Keen Austin as his bride at Old Christ Church. The Reverend William White, rector, and founder of the American Episcopal Church officiated, though Sarah eventually converted to Barry's Catholic faith.

Later in 1777, as the British threatened Philadelphia, Barry had to scuttle the *Effingham*. He then took up command of a smaller craft, the USS *Delaware*. He focused on the destruction of the British hay forage in the region and disrupted shipping in the lower Delaware Bay, often running past British batteries. On March 8, 1778, Barry surprised two British armed sloops and a fortified schooner with seven small craft, including rowboats, barges, and longboats, capturing all three of the enemy vessels.

Later in 1778, Barry was given command of the 32-gun frigate USS *Raleigh* out of Boston. He captured three prizes during this time but learned his beloved brother Patrick was lost at sea with his ship *Union*, which was never heard from after leaving France. Barry's luck also seemed to run out in late September 1778 when the British frigate *Unicorn* and ship-of-the-line *Experiment* chased the *Raleigh* to Penobscot Bay in Maine. For two days, the *Raleigh* battled *Unicorn* until the fore-topmast was cracked. Now in unfamiliar waters, cornered near Wooden Ball Island, Barry planned to save his crew and burn his ship. However, a traitorous crewmember prevented the destruction of the ship and the escape of all the crew. Barry did manage to get away with 88 men, two-thirds of his men, but the *Raleigh* was captured by the British.

While awaiting his next command, Barry wrote a signal book to improve communications between ships at sea. It was published first in 1780.

Barry was next in command of the 36-gun frigate *Alliance* in 1780. That December, he was assigned to convey Colonel John Laurens on a diplomatic mission to join Ben Franklin in France. Laurens was initially reluctant to go, but after being convinced by Alexander Hamilton and the Congress, he arrived on March 1781. Along the way, Barry engaged in battle with and subdued two British sloops of war and captured several prizes.

Barry's most famous naval battle happened off Newfoundland on May 28, 1781. The *Alliance* battled with two British sloops, *Atlanta* and *Trespassey*. The Alliance opened up and gained the initial advantage but was then becalmed. The two sloops managed to get in front and behind *Alliance* and rake her with fire causing considerable damage to the rigging and steerage. Undeterred, Barry continued the defense of his ship until he was struck in the left shoulder by canister projectiles. He continued to lead his men for another twenty minutes until he passed out from the loss of blood. He was then taken below to the ship's surgeon.

After the *Alliance's* flag was shot away, the second in command, Lieutenant Hoysted Hacker, came to Barry while his wounds were being dressed. He urgently requested permission to surrender due to their dire position. Said Barry angrily, "No, Sir, the thunder! If this ship cannot be fought without me, I will be brought on deck. To your duty, Sir."

The crew raised a new flag, and the fight continued. As Hacker returned to the deck, luck turned for the better as the wind picked up.

Washington presents Barry with his commission

This filled *Alliance*'s sails, allowing her to swing about. The following broadsides on the inferior British vessels were devastating, resulting in the surrender of both ships.

This four-hour battle cost the British two ships, one dead captain, eleven dead sailors, and twenty-five wounded. Captain Edwards, the surviving British commander, came to the deck of *Alliance* to surrender, as was customary. He was led to Barry's cabin where he presented his sword. Barry received it, and then returned it saying, "I return it to you, Sir. You have merited it, and your king ought to give you a better ship. Here is my cabin, at your service. Use it as your own."

Barry continued at the helm of *Alliance* for the remainder of the war. While cruising the shipping lanes between Bermuda and Cape Sable, he captured four British ships. Off the Straits of Florida, while returning from Havana on March 1783, he encountered three British frigates seeking to intercept him while he escorted the *Duc de Lauzon* which was transporting 72,000 Spanish pieces of eight bound for the Continental

Congress. Off Cape Canaveral, *Alliance* battled the British frigate, *Sybil*, shattering her rigging, masts, and hull. It was the last naval battle of the war.

In the years immediately after the war, Barry returned to the maritime trade, and from 1787 to 1789 he helped to open commerce to China and the Orient while captaining the merchant ship *Asia*. While the Barrys had no children, they raised their nephews Michael and Patrick Hayes, who had been brought to Philadelphia from Ireland. They were the sons of Barry's deceased sister Eleanor. Young Patrick accompanied his uncle on these journeys to the Far East.

In the 1790s, under the direction of President George Washington, the United States Navy was reinstated in response to trouble with the Barbary Pirates. On June 5, 1794, Secretary of War Henry Knox informed Barry he had been selected senior Captain of the Federal Navy by the President with the advice and consent of the Senate. Barry immediately set about to construct and equip the first frigates of the United States Navy including his flagship 44-gun frigate the USS *United States*. The ship was ready for service in 1797. That year, on February 22, Barry was issued Commission Number 1 by President George Washington, backdated to June 4, 1794, dubbing him "Commodore." Barry was the first commissioned naval officer in the U.S.A. and its first flag officer.

Barry commanded the American fleet during the undeclared Quasi-War with France from 1798 to 1800. He captured several French merchant vessels and transported commissioners William Richardson Davie and Oliver Ellsworth to France to negotiate a new alliance.

Commodore Barry's last action in active service was as the squadron commander at Guadeloupe from 1798 to 1801.

Under the Adams administration, Barry requested a Department of the Navy be formed distinct from the Department of War. This was achieved, and government-funded naval facilities were established.

The popular Barry was so well-regarded President Jefferson retained his services despite reorganizing the military establishment. Barry was also responsible for training many of the naval heroes of the War of 1812, leading his contemporaries to declare him "The Father of the American Navy."

The grave of John Barry

Later in life, Barry was socially active as a member of the Friendly Sons of St. Patrick, the Hibernian Fire Company, and the Society of the Cincinnati. He had also always been a member of the Charitable Captains of Ships Club providing relief to widows and orphans of lost sailors.

Barry remained the head of the United States Navy until his death from complications of asthma on September 12, 1803, at his country home "Strawberry Hill" a few miles outside of Philadelphia. Two days later, he received his country's salute in a full military burial in Philadelphia's Old St. Mary's Churchyard.

Barry was well-regarded by his peers, including John Paul Jones, who bequeathed to Barry, upon his death, the gold sword he had received when knighted by French King Louis XVI. Barry wore the sword during the Quasi-War. When he died, he gave the sword to Jones' favorite lieutenant, Richard Dale. The sword is now displayed at Jones' tomb at the U.S. Navy Academy in Annapolis, Maryland. Barry's Bible is showcased nearby, resting on the altar in the chapel.

Physician and friend Benjamin Rush eulogized Barry: "He fought often and once bled in the cause of freedom, but his habits of war did not lessen in him the peaceful virtues which adorn private life."

Commodore John Barry is memorialized in a multitude of ways:

- The U.S. Revenue Cutter *Commodore Barry.*
- Commodore Barry Park in Brooklyn, New York.
- Four U.S. Navy ships: USS Barry (DD-2) (1902–1920); USS Barry (DD-248) (1921–1945); USS Barry (DD-933) (1956–1983); USS Barry (DDG-52) (1992–present).
- World War II liberty ship SS John Barry.
- A large portrait of Commodore Barry at the Rhode Island State House in Providence.
- Title 16 of the Rhode Island Statutes (§ 16-20-3 – Days of special observance) requires observing September 13 as Commodore John Barry Day.
- Commodore Barry Bridge, which crosses the Delaware River from Chester, Pennsylvania to Bridgeport, New Jersey.
- John Barry Hall at Villanova University.
- Commodore Barry Club (Philadelphia Irish Center) Emlen Street & Carpenter Lane, Mount Airy, Philadelphia, Pennsylvania.
- Barry Township, Schuylkill County, Pennsylvania.
- Commodore John Barry Elementary School in Philadelphia, Pennsylvania.
- Commodore John Barry Elementary School in Chicago, Illinois.
- Commodore John Barry Division of Ancient Order of Hibernians, Annapolis, Maryland.
- John Barry Bar, Grand Hyatt Muscat, Muscat, Oman.
- September 13, Commodore John Barry Day in New Jersey public schools.
- Commodore John Barry Memorial Plaque at Staten Island Borough Hall.
- Plaques at Port Canaveral, Boston Common, and Old St. Mary's Church in Philadelphia.
- A life-sized bronze statue stands in Franklin Square in Washington, D.C.
- Barry Hall is one of six military barracks facilities at the United States Merchant Marine Academy.

- An entrance to the United States Naval Academy commemorates him.
- A large statue of Barry stands directly in front of the formal entrance to Independence Hall in Philadelphia, Pennsylvania.
- A statue of Barry overlooks the Crescent Quay in Wexford town in Ireland. It was a gift to the village from the United States and was delivered by a United States Navy destroyer USS John R. Pierce (DD-753). The statue was unveiled in 1956, and each year a parade and wreath-laying ceremony takes place at the statue to celebrate "Barry Day," commemorated by the Irish Naval Service and the Minister for Defence.

Jacob Broom
(1752–1810)

Surveyor from Delaware

Buried at Christ Episcopal Churchyard,
Philadelphia, Pennsylvania.

———·•·———

U.S. Constitution

———◆◆———

Jacob Broom, from Wilmington, Delaware, was the son of a farmer and blacksmith who assisted the military during the Revolution as a surveyor and became involved in Delaware politics afterward. He was selected to attend the Constitutional Convention and signed the U.S. Constitution.

———◆◆———

Broom was born October 17, 1752, the son of James Broom and Esther Willis Broom from Wilmington, Delaware. The mother was a Quaker, but the younger Broom was later affiliated with the Episcopal Church. James Broom prospered at farming and was also a blacksmith. Young Jacob was likely educated at home and probably at the Old Academy in Wilmington. Broom initially followed his father into farming but also studied surveying and got involved in the mercantile trade and real estate in partnership with his father. On December 14, 1773, he married Rachel Pierce, the daughter of Robert and Elizabeth Pierce, with whom he had eight children.

As a young man of 24, in 1776, Jacob became the assistant burgess (vice mayor) of Wilmington. Over the years, he held numerous local offices including chief burgess four times, borough assessor, and president

Jacob Broom

of the city "street regulators." They oversaw the streets and sewers, laying logs across the roads to assist with drainage. It is said Broom never lost an election in which he campaigned.

Given his mother's pacifist Quaker influence, Jacob did not take up arms directly against England when the Revolutionary War began. Instead, he utilized his surveying skills to assist in the making of maps for the army. There is a record of him doing so for George Washington before the Battle of Brandywine, which occurred about fifteen miles from the Broom homestead on September 11, 1777. The map hung for many years at the Historical Library of Philadelphia at Thirteenth and Locust Streets. It is not known how many other surveys Jacob made for the army.

At the end of the Revolution in 1783, George Washington, having resigned his post as commander of the army, passed through Wilmington on his way to Mount Vernon. Broom spoke in honor of the future president urging him to "contribute your advice and influence to promote that harmony and union of our infant governments which are so essential to the permanent establishment of our freedom, happiness, and prosperity." Washington then followed with a speech of his own in response.

Broom was elected to the Delaware state legislature for the years 1784 to 1786 and 1788. He became involved in national politics when he was selected to attend the Annapolis Convention to discuss trade between the states. This meeting was a precursor to the Constitutional Convention and was poorly attended. Broom did not go either.

In 1786, the president of the Delaware Assembly, Nickolas Van Dyke, appointed Broom justice of the peace for New Castle County. The next year, Broom was asked to be one of the Delaware representatives at the Constitutional Convention in Philadelphia along with George Read, John Dickinson, Gunning Bedford, and Richard Bassett. Broom attended all the sessions and consistently voted for measures related to a stable central government, aligned with the Federalists. Regarding Senators, he favored a single nine-year term with equal representation from the states. He wanted the states to pay their representatives in Congress and would give those representatives the power to veto state laws. He viewed the office of President as an appointment for life and wanted the state legislatures to select the presidential electors. While Broom held strong opinions, he rarely spoke, permitting other more influential and experienced delegates to make his points. Georgia delegate William Pierce described Broom as "a plain good Man, with some abilities, but nothing to render him conspicuous. He is silent in public, but cheerful and conversable in private." Broom signed the U.S. Constitution on behalf of Delaware, which was the first state to ratify it on December 7, 1787.

Back home in Wilmington under the new republic, Broom became the first postmaster general for Wilmington, holding the post from 1790 to 1792.

He erected a new home and cotton mill in 1795 on the Brandywine Creek, on the outskirts of Wilmington near the village of Montchanin. This house, called "Hagley," still stands and is a historic landmark known as the Jacob Broom House. In 1802, after a fire took the mill, he sold the property mill to Éleuthère Irénée du Pont, a French immigrant. Du Pont built his gunpowder mill on the property and used the house as

The grave of Jacob Broom

his residence and business headquarters. The property was subsequently incorporated into the Hagley Museum and Library.

Broom chaired the board of directors for Wilmington's Delaware Bank. He was also involved in other pursuits such as a machine shop that repaired mill machinery, a failed scheme to mine bog iron ore, and improvements to toll roads, canals, and bridges.

Broom was deeply religious and was a leader at the Old Swedes Church in Wilmington. He was also involved in the reorganization of the Old Academy into the College of Wilmington. He served on the first board of trustees. This institution later became incorporated into the University of Delaware.

Broom died in 1810 at the age of 57 while on a business trip to nearby Philadelphia. He was buried at the Christ Episcopal Churchyard. The exact location of his grave is unknown.

In 1987, the Delaware State Society of the Daughters of the American Revolution placed a cenotaph there in his honor.

Broom Street in Madison, Wisconsin is named after Jacob Broom.

Pierce Butler
(1744–1822)

The British Soldier Who Became a Founder

Buried at Christ Episcopal Churchyard,
Philadelphia, Pennsylvania.

— ·•·—

U.S. Constitution • Military

This founder proudly pointed out that he was a descendant of the Duke of Ormond. Born to the British aristocracy, he chose to pursue a military life. He was a major in the British army when he arrived in America with his majesty's forces to fight in the French and Indian War. Later troops under his command fired the shots at what came to be known as the Boston Massacre. He was, however, among many British soldiers who liked what they saw in the new world: plenty of land, easy access to clean running water, and numerous orchards that appealed to the planter in him. By 1773 he had resigned his commission in the army, married, and moved to Charleston. When the Revolution began, he found himself fighting on the patriot side. He became active in South Carolina politics and represented his state at the Constitutional Convention where he played an active part and signed the finished product. His name was Pierce Butler.

—►·◄—

Butler was born on July 11, 1744, in County Carlow, Ireland. He was the third son born to Sir Richard Butler, 5th Baronet of Cloughgrenan, and his wife, Henrietta Percy. As one of the younger sons born to wealthy aristocrats, Butler had little chance of inheriting his father's wealth. He did have the advantage of quality education, including according to the

Pierce Butler

historian Clinton Rossiter "working knowledge of the law." In young Butler's view, he had a choice to either pursue a life in the church or the military, and he decided on the latter. It was the French and Indian War that brought him to the country that would become his home.

In 1771 Butler married Mary Middleton, the daughter of Thomas Middleton and niece of Declaration of Independence signer Arthur Middleton. Shortly after his marriage he resigned his commission in the British army and decided to take up the life of a planter in the Charleston area. It was here he hoped to live the life of a gentleman farmer. The Revolution would interrupt those plans.

In the early years of the American revolt against British rule, military action was centered mainly in the northern and middle colonies. In 1778 the Crown's forces decided to pursue a "southern strategy" in the hope that loyalists in the southern states would rally in support of the British troops. By this time Butler had been elected to the state legislature and at the request of South Carolina Governor John Rutledge assumed the post as the state's adjutant general. This position carried with it the title of brigadier general though Butler preferred being addressed as major, which had been his combat rank.

Butler helped organize the South Carolina militia to prepare for the expected British invasion. He was also active in Georgia where he served under General Lachlan McIntosh. The troops the duo hastily raised and just as quickly trained could not stand against the British regulars and the effort to relieve Savannah ended in failure for the patriot side. In 1780 the British conquered Charleston, South Carolina, and Butler joined a resistance movement that included the "Swamp Fox" Francis Marion. Being a former British officer, Butler represented a special target for his majesty's forces, and he barely avoided capture on multiple occasions. He also aided the American effort by personally donating both money and supplies to the army in which he now served.

The British did confiscate Butler's property, including his slaves. When the Revolution ended in victory, he traveled to the Netherlands and, using his land as collateral, obtained a sizable loan from the Dutch. He used this money to purchase both slaves and equipment to resume his life as a planter. Several bad harvests nearly ruined him, and only a law passed by the South Carolina legislature saved his property from being seized by his creditors. It probably didn't hurt that he was a member of the body that passed the law that brought him relief.

In 1787 Butler joined the South Carolina delegation as a representative to the Constitutional Convention in Philadelphia. He was a very active member of the gathering who attended every meeting and spoke approximately seventy times. He also proposed the secrecy rule that the delegates adopted. Later James Madison would say that "no Constitution would ever have been adopted by the convention if the debates had been public." While Butler came to favor the establishment of the strong federal government proposed by Madison, he tempered that support by opposing any measures that would have limited slavery under the new government. He also joined fellow South Carolinian Charles Pinckney in proposing a requirement that fugitive slaves be returned to their owners. Not a single member of the convention voted against that proposal and many credit Butler with being the man responsible for the Constitution's fugitive slave clause.

As a delegate to the Philadelphia Convention Butler favored requiring only nine states for adoption rather than eleven. Butler "revolted at

The grave of Pierce Butler

the idea that one or two states should restrain the others from consulting their safety." Though Butler strongly supported the ratification of the U.S. Constitution, he did not take part in his state's convention.

He did represent his state in the first Congress serving as a United States Senator for three terms. When political parties began to form Butler first joined the Federalist ranks, but by 1795 he had switched sides and joined the party favoring Thomas Jefferson. In 1804 he declared himself an independent. That same year he hosted Vice President Aaron Burr at one of his plantations. Burr had just killed Alexander Hamilton in a duel and was laying low after having been indicted for murder in both New York and New Jersey.

The years following the Constitutional Convention were also good ones for Butler financially. Bountiful harvests had turned him into one of the wealthiest men in America. When his wife died in 1790, he sold his holdings in South Carolina and invested in Georgia sea island plantations. He also purchased homes in Philadelphia and, during his last years, moved there to be closer to his daughter. He passed away in the City of Brotherly Love in 1822 at the age of 77 and was laid to rest at the Christ Church Episcopal Churchyard.

William Clingan
(1721–1790)

Chester County Continental Congressman

Buried at Upper Octorara Church Cemetery,
Parkesburg, Pennsylvania.

————•—•————

Articles of Confederation

William Clingan was a Continental Congressman born circa 1721 who attended the Congress from 1777 to 1779, including the months when it met in Lancaster and then York, Pennsylvania during the British occupation of Philadelphia. During this time, Clingan signed the Articles of Confederation which was later ratified by the states in 1781.

Born near Wagontown in Caln Township, Chester County, Pennsylvania, Clingan was likely the son of immigrants from Northern Ireland or Scotland. His educational details are lost to history, but he did marry twice: first to Catherine (maiden name unknown) with whom he had a son before her death in 1785; and second to Rachel Gilleylen (1756-1843), a widow with six children from her first marriage, who survived him.

Clingan owned hundreds of acres of land in the Wagontown area and resided along the King's Highway from Philadelphia to Lancaster, the current Route 340, just west of Wagontown. The current address for the property is 101 Hatfield Road, Coatesville, Pennsylvania. From 1757 to 1786, he served as a justice of the peace in Chester County and, for the last six years, President of the Chester County Courts.

William Clingan

William Clingan was elected to the Continental Congress as a delegate from Pennsylvania on September 14, 1777. He attended sessions from November 1 to about November 28, 1777; from January 1, 1778 to about March 24, 1778; from about April 25, 1778, to about May 19, 1778; from about June 16, 1778 to about June 27, 1778; and from about September 14, 1778 to about December 2, 1778. He was re-elected on November 20, 1778.

These dates of service put William Clingan in the room for the final debates on the Articles of Confederation and then the adoption on November 15, 1777, in York. Beginning on July 9, 1778, the delegates began signing the document. Along with Clingan, Robert Morris, Daniel Roberdeau, Jonathan Bayard Smith, and Joseph Reed signed for Pennsylvania.

William Clingan's nephew and namesake married Jane Roan, the beautiful daughter of revered pastor John Roan and his wife Anne, on June 11, 1778. Jane's uncle John Cochran was a distinguished surgeon in the Revolutionary army. The wedding was noteworthy enough to receive a lot of coverage in *The Pennsylvania Packet* newspaper:

Was married, last Thursday, Mr. William Clingan, Jr., of Donegal, to Miss Jenny Roan, of Londonderry, both of the County of Lancaster—a sober, sensible, agreeable young couple and very sincere Whigs. This marriage promises as much happiness as the state of things in this our sinful world will admit.

This was indeed a Whig wedding, as there were present many young men and ladies, and not one of the gentlemen but had been out when called on in the service of his country, and it was well-known that the groom, in particular, had proved his heroism, as well as Whiggism, in several battles and skirmishes. After the marriage was ended, a motion was made, and heartily agreed to by all present, that the young unmarried ladies should form themselves into an association by the name of the "Whig Association of the Unmarried Ladies of America," in which they should pledge their honor that they would never give their hand in marriage to any gentleman until he had first proved himself a patriot, in readily turning out when called to defend his country from slavery, by a spirited and brave conduct, as they would not wish to be the mothers of a race of slaves and cowards.

The younger Clingan was a soldier who participated in the battles at Trenton, Princeton, Brandywine, and Germantown and had served in the army elsewhere. The couple later moved northwest to the Buffalo Valley near Lewisburg, Pennsylvania.

Following his service in Congress, the elder Clingan returned to his duties on the court in Chester County. He was a Justice of the Peace for the district of West Caln, Sadsbury, and West Fallowfield Townships, and Justice of the Court of Common Pleas of Chester County. He also presided in the Court of Quarter Sessions and the Orphans' Court there. Clingan was instrumental in the planning and construction of a new prison and court facilities in Chester County.

The grave of William Clingan

Throughout his life, William was a leading member of the Upper Octorara Presbyterian Church, which is along present-day Route 10 near Parkesburg, Pennsylvania. According to an early *History of Chester County, Pennsylvania*, Clingan was robbed of the church collections:

At one time during the career of the noted robbers, the Doanes, Mr. Clingan was visited by them. In some business transactions, he had received a large amount of money in gold, and the visit of the Doanes had reference to this treasure, which they supposed was in the house. While searching for it, one of them announced that he had found it. Mr. Clingan's desk had been opened, and there stood a large leathern bag full of money, and seizing a violin which was in the house, as they said, to have a jubilation over their good luck, they mounted their horses and were off. The bag, however, which they supposed to contain the gold was simply filled with coppers, the church collections as he had brought them home from Sunday to Sunday, and which, when he had a quantity on hand, he exchanged for larger money. One of the gang, afterward executed, was visited by Mr. Clingan in prison, and he told him of their chagrin when they discovered their mistake.

William Clingan died on May 9, 1790, and was laid to rest in the Upper Octorara Burial Grounds. His tombstone reads:

Here lyeth the Body of WILLIAM CLINGAN, Esq. Who departed this Life, The 9th Day of May 1790. Also CATHERINE, his Wife, Who departed this Life, The 8th Day of Feby 1785.

William Clingan left no descendants.

George Clymer
(1739–1813)

A Pennsylvania Patriot

Buried at Friends' Burying Ground,
Trenton, New Jersey.

—————•◦•—————

Declaration of Independence • U.S. Constitution

George Clymer of Pennsylvania was an early proponent of independence from Great Britain. He was one of only five people who signed both the Declaration of Independence and the Constitution. He was a Continental Congressman and a member of the First Congress of the United States in 1789.

—————◦•◦—————

Clymer was born in Philadelphia on March 16, 1739, to Christopher Clymer and Deborah (née Fitzwater) Clymer. Christopher was a ship's captain who had emigrated from Bristol, England. He was the son of Richard Clymer of Bristol. Deborah's parents were George Fitzwater and Mary Hardiman, Quakers from Philadelphia. Christopher Clymer died in 1740. Deborah followed a few years later or possibly remarried leaving George an orphan at an early age.

Orphaned George was sent to live with his mother's sister and her husband, Hannah and William Coleman. Coleman was a wealthy merchant who was a leader among the Quakers, also known as the Society of Friends. Coleman saw to Clymer's education and George followed in Coleman's footsteps as a merchant. In his 20s, Clymer worked in Coleman's counting house and with Reese Meredith in 1764. Soon Meredith and Clymer

George Clymer

became business partners. Clymer married Reese Meredith's daughter Elizabeth in 1765, further cementing the business arrangements. The couple had nine children, five of whom lived to adulthood.

George Clymer joined the patriot cause around the time of the Sugar Act (1764) and the Stamp Act (1765). As a leader in the Philadelphia business community, he signed the nonimportation agreement that stymied trade with Britain and led to the repeal of the Stamp Act in 1766.

William Coleman died in 1769, leaving a large inheritance to Clymer. At the age of 39, Clymer was now independently wealthy and entered the political realm. He was elected to Philadelphia's City Council and was later a justice and an alderman. Following the British response to the Boston Tea Party in 1774, Clymer joined Pennsylvania's Committee of Correspondence calling for a meeting in Philadelphia that would become the First Continental Congress. He was named to the Congress and became the Continental Treasurer in July 1775, sharing the duties with Michael Hillegas. In November 1775, Clymer was appointed to the Pennsylvania Committee of Safety which took control of the government of Pennsylvania and saw to its defense.

Some of the initial delegates from Pennsylvania who were asked to sign the Declaration of Independence refused to do so, including John Dickinson, Andrew Allen, Charles Humphreys, and Thomas Willing. On July 20, 1776, Clymer, along with George Ross, Benjamin Rush, George Taylor, and James Wilson, were all elected to the Continental Congress with the express purpose of signing the Declaration. They did so, and though Clymer was late to sign it, "[he] affixed his signature to the manifesto, as if in the performance of an act which was about to consummate his dearest wishes, and realize those fond prospects of national prosperity which had ever been transcendent in his thoughts."

Clymer continued in his service as a Continental Congressman, visiting the army at Ticonderoga in September of 1776, and participating through 1777 and then 1780-1782. During this time, he also was a delegate to Pennsylvania's Constitutional Convention and helped form the Bank of Pennsylvania with Robert Morris. Morris and Clymer were then co-directors of the Bank of North America starting in 1781.

In 1787, Clymer, along with Ben Franklin and James Wilson, was named as Pennsylvania delegates to the Constitutional Convention. George was focused on the financial aspects of the proceedings including the assumption of war debts by the central government. Clymer was a strong proponent for a bicameral legislature. Upon ratification, Clymer was elected to the First Congress (1789-1791) but did not seek a second term.

Back in Pennsylvania, Clymer was the head of the Pennsylvania Department of Excise Taxes. When the Whiskey Rebellion broke out in defiance to whiskey taxes, Meredith Clymer, George's son, was among the military force that put down the insurrection. In a stroke of incredibly bad luck young Clymer was one of the few militiamen killed by the rebels. The elder Clymer was devastated and resigned his post. His last public service was at the end of Washington's second term in 1796 when the first president named Clymer to a panel that negotiated peace with the Creek and Cherokee nations in Georgia. A treaty was completed by the next year.

The grave of George Clymer

Through his remaining years, Clymer focused on philanthropic pursuits, raising funds for the University of Pennsylvania and serving as the president of the Pennsylvania Academy of Fine Arts. He served as president of the Philadelphia Society for Promoting Agriculture from 1805 to 1813. He was also president of the Philadelphia Bank from 1803 until his death.

George Clymer died at his son Henry's home in Morrisville, Pennsylvania, just across the Delaware River from Trenton, New Jersey, on January 23, 1813. He was 73 years old. None of the obituaries mentioned his signing of our nation's most important documents. He was laid to rest at the Friends' Burying Ground in Trenton, New Jersey, despite not being the place where he was born, lived, served, or died. He has a very simple grave that borders a parking lot.

Tench Coxe
(1755–1824)

Economist & Opportunist

Buried at Christ Church Burial Ground,
Philadelphia, Pennsylvania.

Continental Congress • Revenue Commissioner

Tench Coxe was an American political economist and served in several political offices including as a delegate for Pennsylvania to the Continental Congress. Coxe proved to be one of the nation's more controversial founders. He is remembered more for his work on behalf of commercial and trade issues than for his political work. He is best known as an economic writer who preached a brand of mercantilism that elevated manufacturing to a prominent role. He never achieved the position or acceptance he so desired and never understood that those from whom he sought rewards doubted his loyalty, consistency, and objectivity. He was called "Mr. Facing Bothways" by many of his contemporaries.

Tench Coxe was born in Philadelphia, Pennsylvania on May 22, 1755, into a family that continually held a leading role in public affairs. He was named for his maternal grandfather Tench Francis, a leading attorney in Pennsylvania, who served as the Attorney General of Pennsylvania in 1741. His parents were William Coxe and Mary Coxe and were landowners.

Young Tench received his education in the Philadelphia schools and entered the Philadelphia College and Academy (now the University of

Tench Coxe

Pennsylvania) in 1771 at the age of 16. By the end of 1772, he had left school and become a merchant in Philadelphia, opening his own trading house. He thought of studying law, but his father urged him to join his commercial concern. In 1776, amid the revolution, he joined Coxe, Furman, and Coxe as a partner. He was more interested in business than politics.

At one point in 1776, he enlisted in the 4th Pennsylvania Regiment but quickly decided he did not want to fight and resigned his commission. When his name became associated with Loyalists who were siding with the British against the American cause, Coxe panicked and fled to New York City, then under British control. When the British raided Pennsylvania and seized control of Philadelphia, forcing the Continental Congress to flee, Coxe marched alongside the British troops into the city on September 26, 1777. The British held Philadelphia for a time while Continental forces tried several attempts to force them out including battles at Brandywine and Germantown. During this time, Coxe was able to go about his business, making a tidy profit from the increased British business.

When the British were forced to flee from Philadelphia in 1778, Coxe remained. Some Patriots accused him of having Loyalist sympathies and having served in the British Army. For some reason, no harm came to him. His trading successes during the period of British occupation lent considerable support to the charges, yet nothing came of the allegations.

When the revolution ended, Coxe formed the international merchant firm of Coxe and Frazier and began to take an interest in politics. In 1778 his first wife Catherine McCall died suddenly, and in 1782 Coxe married his first cousin Rebecca Coxe, with whom he had ten children. By this time he was an extremely wealthy man. One of his many civic activities was serving as secretary of the Pennsylvania Society for Promoting the Abolition of Slavery, of which Benjamin Franklin was president. In 1786, Coxe represented Pennsylvania by serving as the secretary for the Annapolis Convention, the effort to revise the ineffective Articles of Confederation, which set the stage for the Constitutional Convention the next year.

In the summer of 1787, while the Constitutional Convention met in Philadelphia, Coxe presented a paper urging industrial development to the Society for Political Enquiries at Ben Franklin's house. He became a Whig and published three articles in the *Philadelphia Independent Gazetteer* that fall. The articles examined the new U.S. Constitution and compared it favorably to the British Constitution.

In 1788 Coxe served as one of Pennsylvania's last delegates to the Constitutional Convention. According to historian Edmund Cody Burnett, Coxe attended the Congress for a single day, January 10, 1789. On March 3, the Continental Congress was dissolved, and the following day the new U.S. Congress came into being.

Coxe next became a Federalist and was appointed as the Assistant Secretary of the Treasury by Alexander Hamilton. As the Assistant Secretary, Coxe gathered research that Hamilton used to promote manufacturing. They co-authored the famous "Report on Manufactures" in 1791. In 1792, Hamilton made Coxe the Commissioner of the Revenue

The grave of Tench Coxe

in charge of the collection of all tax revenues. He served in that role until removed by President John Adams.

Coxe then turned Democratic-Republican, and President Thomas Jefferson appointed him Purveyor of Public Supplies. In that role, he was responsible for procuring arms for the standing army and the militias. He served in that capacity from 1803 to 1812.

Coxe retired from public service in 1818 after having served three years as Clerk of The Quarter Sessions in Philadelphia. He spent his remaining years as a writer. He championed tariffs to protect the nations growing industries and the second amendment right to bear arms. It should be noted that firearms were among the many commodities dealt in for many years by the firm of Coxe and Frazier.

Tench Coxe died on July 17, 1824, in Philadelphia. He is buried in Christ Church Burial Ground.

John Dickinson
(1732–1808)

Penman of the Revolution

Buried at Friends Meeting House Burial Grounds,
Wilmington, Delaware.

**Thought Leader • Military • Articles of Confederation
U.S. Constitution**

This founder favored reconciliation with the mother country as opposed to declaring American Independence. As a delegate from Pennsylvania to the Continental Congress, he abstained on the vote for independence. He also declined to sign the document that declared it. After his fellow delegates passed that motion, he left Congress and joined the Continental Army and fought in the Revolution. Despite not favoring independence he had worked with Thomas Jefferson on a document titled *A Declaration of the Causes and Necessity of Taking Up Arms*. He also authored *Letters from a Farmer in Pennsylvania* in which he argued that the English Parliament did not have the authority to tax the colonies. These writings earned him the title "Penman of the Revolution." Thus his writings were seen to have ignited the fires for a cause that he refused to endorse. During his life, he served as the president of two states Pennsylvania and Delaware, and he represented the latter at the 1787 Constitutional Convention. His signature is also affixed to the document produced by that gathering. Thomas Jefferson called him a true patriot, and he was undoubtedly a man known to stand by his principles regardless of the cost. His name was John Dickinson.

Dickinson was born on or around November 8, 1732, on his family's tobacco plantation, which was located in Maryland. His father had inherited the estate of 2,500 acres which he expanded to 9,000 acres. He also purchased land in Delaware where he started another plantation and christened it Poplar Hall. These were profitable ventures that were worked using slave labor until 1777 when the subject of this chapter freed the slaves of Poplar Hall.

In his youth, Dickinson was educated at his home by tutors. The most important of these was William Killen, who became the lifelong friend of his student. Killen himself would become Delaware's first Chief Justice and Chancellor. At the age of 18, Dickinson began the study of law under John Milan in Philadelphia. He also spent three years in England to continue those studies before being admitted to the Pennsylvania Bar in 1757.

By 1770 Dickinson was a successful lawyer and one of the wealthiest men in the colonies. That year he married Mary "Polly" Norris whose father was the Speaker of the Pennsylvania General Assembly. Dickinson's wife would inherit 500 acres in Carlisle, Pennsylvania that the couple would donate to John and Mary's College in 1784. The College was renamed Dickinson College. Thus he was bestowed the honor of having an institution of higher learning named in his honor while he still walked the earth.

The Norris family were Quakers as the Dickinson's had been until a dispute with the sect over a family marriage led to a break with the Quaker society. Though Dickinson himself never became an active Quaker, he believed in many Quaker principles though not pacifism since he did not object to a defensive war. It was this belief that allowed him to join the Continental Army and fight in defense of the newly formed United States.

After his wedding, Dickinson's political career blossomed. It was during this period that he enhanced his reputation throughout the colonies through his writings, as mentioned earlier, that were critical of the English Parliament's imposition of the Townshend Acts. Dickinson wrote that while the English government could regulate commerce, they had no authority to tax. He warned his fellow citizens that accepting the

John Dickinson

Townshend Acts would result in other taxes being levied on the colonies in the future.

In 1774 Dickinson was selected to represent Pennsylvania in the Continental Congress. It was here that he urged his fellow delegates to pursue a peaceful solution with England. It was his view that independence was not in the best interests of the colonies. His arguments failed to convince Congress, and when the vote was conducted on July 2, 1776, to declare independence, he abstained. He felt that standing by his convictions would be detrimental to his political future. He said, "My conduct this day, I expect will give the finishing blow to my once too great and, my integrity considered, now too diminished popularity."

Though he refused to sign the declaration, during his lifetime, Dickinson was recognized as a significant influence on the subject based on his previous writings. As a matter of fact, in 1787, Thomas Jefferson read an article in the *Journal de Paris* that put forth the position that it was the influence of Dickinson that resulted in the adoption of American independence. Jefferson wrote a long letter to the editor in which he insisted that Dickinson was on the other side of the question and would point out the error in the article himself if given a chance. The author of the declaration never mailed the letter which was discovered among his papers after his death. Some have theorized that Jefferson didn't have the letter delivered because it would appear as self-serving even though he makes clear that its purpose was to correct the historical record.

Leaving Congress, Dickinson accepted a position as a Brigadier General in the Pennsylvania militia. In this position, he commanded 10,000 troops which were dispatched to Elizabeth, New Jersey in anticipation of a British attack. After being passed over by promotions that went to two junior officers, Dickinson resigned his commission and returned to Poplar Hall in Delaware. It was here that he learned that his home in Philadelphia had been confiscated by the British and turned into a hospital. Some believe that Dickinson's failure to support independence resulted in the decision on promotions that prompted his resignation.

It appears that Dickinson's fears that refusing to sign the Declaration would result in a significant loss of public support were unfounded. In 1777 the Delaware General Assembly tried to send him back to the Continental Congress, but he refused to serve. Instead, he served as a private in the Kent County Militia under Caesar Rodney. When his friend Thomas McKean tried to promote him to the post of Brigadier General of the Delaware Militia he again declined to serve in that capacity. It was during this period that Dickinson freed the 37 slaves who worked at Poplar Hall.

In 1779 Dickinson agreed to represent Delaware in the Continental Congress. As a member of this group, he signed the Articles of Confederation which was a document he had worked on as a Pennsylvania delegate in 1776. He left Congress in 1781 after learning that a loyalist raid had severely damaged Poplar Hall. Back in Kent County, he was elected to represent that area in the State Senate. Shortly after taking his seat the General Assembly elected him to the office of President of Delaware. Less than a year later he was also elected to the Supreme Executive Council of Pennsylvania. When the Pennsylvania General Assembly elected him president of the council, he became the State President of both Delaware and Pennsylvania simultaneously.

The modest grave of John Dickinson

In 1787 Dickinson was among Delaware's representatives at the Constitutional Convention. He played an essential role there. Dickinson aided in the development of the Great Compromise which resulted in seats in the House of Representatives being based on population while each state received two seats in the United States Senate. Sick and ailing as the Convention reached its end he returned to Delaware but directed George Read to affix his name to the Constitution. Though he had opportunities to serve in the government established by the Constitution, Dickinson declined. Some believe he made this decision because he had experienced enough of the strains of public life in the years between the Stamp Act Congress and the Constitutional Convention. He left the world of politics entirely in 1793 after serving a final term in the Delaware Senate.

Dickinson lived until 1808. He spent the final 15 years of his life working on the abolition of slavery while making significant donations to organizations working in Dickinson's words to the "relief of the unhappy." He passed away at the age of 75 and was laid to rest in the Friends Meeting House Burial Ground located in Wilmington, Delaware. Responding to Dickinson's passing, Thomas Jefferson wrote, "A more estimable man, or a truer patriot, could not have left us. Among the first of the advocates for the rights of his country when assailed by Great Britain, he continued to the last the orthodox advocate of the true principles of our new government and his name will be consecrated in history as one of the worthies of the Revolution."

William Henry Drayton
(1742 – 1779)

Died in Philadelphia

Buried at Christ Church Burial Grounds,
Philadelphia, Pennsylvania.
In 1979, soil from the grave reburied at Drayton Hall,
Charleston, South Carolina.

Articles of Confederation

This founder initially opposed the growing colonial resistance to British rule after the Stamp Act. As a matter of fact he wrote a series of articles defending the actions taken by England. When these articles were published in Europe he was appointed as a member of the Colonial Council in 1772. Over the next two years his views on colonial rule changed drastically and in 1774 he authored a pamphlet titled the *American Claim of Rights* which supported the call for a Continental Congress. As a result he was removed from his government position which only served to strengthen his views on the rebel cause. During the revolution he represented South Carolina in the Continental Congress. As a member of that Congress he signed the Articles of Confederation. He died before reaching the age of forty and before the end of the Revolution. He remains one of our lesser-known founders. His name was William Henry Drayton.

Drayton was born in the month of September in 1742 at his father's plantation, Drayton Hall, located on the banks of the Ashley River near

William Henry Drayton

Charleston, South Carolina. His birth took place shortly after his father completed construction of the main house located on the large rice plantation. His mother was Charlotta Bull Drayton the daughter of the colony's governor William Bull. His well-connected family sent him to England in 1750 for his education. He attended the Westminster School and Balliol College, Oxford before returning to America in 1764. Upon his return, he studied law and was admitted to the South Carolina bar.

As mentioned above, Drayton's conversion to the American cause was not complete until the mid-1770s. By 1775, he was a member of South Carolina's Committee of Safety and the provisional Congress that functioned as the rebel government of South Carolina. In 1776, he was appointed to the position of Chief Justice on his state's Supreme Court. That same year Drayton raised two battalions to fight in the war against England. South Carolina sent him to Georgia for the purpose of proposing that Georgia, with its smaller population, would benefit by being annexed to its eastern neighbor. Though the proposal was debated, Georgia rejected the idea. A year later, Drayton appealed directly to the citizens

Plaque honoring William Henry Drayton at Christ Church Burial
Ground in Philadelphia, Pennsylvania

of Georgia attempting to convince them of the advantages of joining
South Carolina. This resulted in Georgia's governor offering a reward of
100 pounds for the capture of Drayton. Though he accused the governor
of "nonsense and falsehoods," Drayton returned to South Carolina and
abandoned the effort to annex the neighboring state.

In 1778, South Carolina sent Drayton to Philadelphia as a representative in the Continental Congress. As a member of Congress, he
was a strong supporter of the military and a signer of the Articles of
Confederation. Drayton didn't live long enough to see the Articles ratified or the revolution he championed succeed. While serving in Congress
he passed away from typhus on September 3, 1779. He was laid to rest
in Philadelphia's Christ Church Burial Ground in a now unknown location. In 1979 dust from what was believed to be his grave was taken to
Drayton Hall in South Carolina.

On September 25, 1779, the *Virginia Gazette* reported Drayton's
death. The paper noted that Drayton had been honored by his country
through his appointment to the "most important and confidential offices." The report went on to say that at the time of his death he was Chief
Justice of his state and one of its representatives in Congress. The paper

also proclaimed that Drayton's writings were well-known and studied in both America and Europe. Since he passed away before he reached the age of forty, there is little doubt that had he lived he would have made an even greater mark on the young country he well represented. His past service and reputation would have assured him a voice as the new nation found its footing after the war with England was won.

Thomas Fitzsimons
(1741–1811)

The Irish Founder

Buried at St. Mary's Catholic Church Cemetery,
Philadelphia, Pennsylvania.

**Continental Congress • U.S. Constitution
U.S. House of Representatives**

Thomas Fitzsimons is one of the most obscure founders. Very few people recognize his name. He never sought the limelight but was willing to play a subordinate role to other key figures. He came to America from Ireland to escape horrible conditions and once here faced personal tragedy but rose above it and achieved great success and wealth as a merchant in Philadelphia. His support for independence from Britain took many forms and led him to be a delegate to the Constitutional Convention, a signer of the Constitution and a member of the U.S. House of Representatives for its first three sessions.

Thomas Fitzsimons was born in Ballykilty in County Cork, Ireland in 1741. It was probably the worst time in Ireland's history to be born there. The 1740 -1741 period is known as the Year of Slaughter. The famine is estimated to have killed about 20% of the total population of 2.4 million. This was proportionally greater than during the Great Famine of 1845-1852. Thomas' father is said to have seen fifty babies get buried in the local cemetery outside St. Catherine's Church as starvation

Thomas Fitzsimons

took hold. It took until 1760 for Thomas and his six siblings and father to arrange for passage to America. Tragically once they did arrive in Philadelphia, Thomas' father died. He was said to be sick and weakened because he gave most of his food ration to his children to ensure their survival.

Thomas was smart and hardworking and started working for merchants in Philadelphia. He married Catherine Meade on November 23, 1761, and formed a business partnership with her brother George. The firm of George Meade and Company soon became one of the leading commercial houses in the city and would successfully operate for over 41 years.

Young Thomas Fitzsimons was thrust into politics when in 1771 he was elected first vice-president of the Friendly Sons of St. Patrick, a politically powerful fraternal association. When Parliament reacted to the 1773 Boston Tea Party with punitive measures, which Americans called the Coercive Acts, Philadelphia merchants were infuriated. They felt that if the British could close the port of Boston, no city in America was safe. In 1774 he was elected to a steering committee organized to direct the protest over the Coercive Acts and to the city's Committee of Correspondence, the patriots' shadow government. In choosing him for these positions, the voters ignored a law that barred Catholics from elective office.

When Pennsylvania began mobilizing and organizing a militia to fight the British, Fitzsimons like many immigrants demonstrated his devotion to his adopted land by springing to its defense. He served as a captain of a company he raised in Colonel John Cadwalader's 3rd Battalion. During the summer of 1776, Fitzsimons' company served in the cordon of outposts that under Colonel John Dickinson guarded the New Jersey shoreline. In November, the British invaded New Jersey, and Washington began a slow withdrawal to the Pennsylvania side of the Delaware River. On December 5, Fitzsimons's company went on duty to cover the Continentals retreat by guarding the river's Pennsylvania shore. This company was supposed to be an essential part of Washington's surprise attack on Trenton on Christmas night, but because of deteriorating weather, they were unable to cross the river. They joined Washington several days later in time to deal with a British counterattack. Later in the war, Fitzsimons served on the Pennsylvania Council of Safety and headed a board to oversee the newly formed Pennsylvania Navy.

This experience in the Revolutionary War convinced Fitzsimons of the need for central control of the nation's military forces. His wartime association with Robert Morris convinced him that a reliable and effective national government was essential for the prosperity of the country. His reputation as a caring officer as well as his work for the poor on numerous relief committees made him very popular. He was elected to the Continental Congress in 1782. There he concentrated on financial and commercial matters working closely with Morris and aligned with Alexander Hamilton and James Madison. Frustrated by the constant conflict and criticism, he resigned in 1783.

In 1786 he began the first of three terms in the state House of Representatives. In 1787 the state selected Fitzsimons to represent it

The grave of Thomas Fitzsimons

at the constitutional convention along with Thomas Mifflin, Robert Morris, George Clymer, Jared Ingersoll, James Wilson, Gouverneur Morris, and Ben Franklin. Prior to the convention he often spoke on issues relating to commerce and finance, arguing that the central government should have the right to tax both exports and imports to raise revenue and regulate commerce—a position that he had advocated with little success in the Continental Congress. Although not a leading member at that convention, he supported a strong national government, the end of slavery, and granting the House equal powers with the Senate in making treaties. He was not a supporter of universal suffrage. He was one of only two Catholic signers of the United States Constitution, the other being Daniel Carroll of Maryland.

After the Convention Fitzsimons resumed his serving in the Pennsylvania legislature. There he led the fight for a special convention to ratify the Constitution, arguing that since the document derived its power from the people, the people must approve it through representatives elected solely for that purpose.

After the Constitution was established, he served in the first three sessions of the House of Representatives as a Federalist. He was Chairman of the Ways and Means Committee. He co-sponsored the law that authorized the original six frigates of the United States Navy. He failed to win re-election in 1794. He devoted the rest of his life to business and charitable affairs. He served as President of Philadelphia's Chamber of Commerce and as a trustee of the University of Pennsylvania.

Fitzsimons died on August 26, 1811, at the age of 70. His tomb is in the graveyard at St. Mary's Roman Catholic Church which is in present Independence National Historical Park.

Edward Hand
(1744–1802)

Lancaster's Major General

Buried at St. James Episcopal Church Cemetery,
Lancaster, Pennsylvania.

Military • Continental Congress

Edward Hand was born and raised in Ireland and first came to America as a doctor in the British army. He was sympathetic to the American cause and enlisted in the Continental Army where he had an illustrious career rising to retire as a Major General. He served with George Washington at the battle of Trenton and served as Adjutant General during the Battle of Yorktown. He later was elected to the Continental Congress and the Pennsylvania Assembly and was a delegate to the Pennsylvania Constitutional Convention.

Edward Hand was born December 31, 1744, in Clyduff, Kings County (now County Offaly) in central Ireland. He was educated at Trinity College in Dublin where he studied medicine. He decided to put his medical training to use by joining the British army as a surgeon's mate and was assigned to the 18th Royal Irish Regiment of Foot.

He and his regiment set sail from Cobh, County Cork, on May 20, 1767, and arrived in Philadelphia on July 11, 1767. He was 23 years old when he arrived in the colonies and was assigned to Fort Pitt. Along with his regiment, he marched west from Philadelphia to the fort located where the city of Pittsburgh sits today.

Edward Hand

Fort Pitt was, at the time, one of the key defensive positions and one of the most imposing, complex, and elaborate British installations in the Americas.

Hand would remain at Fort Pitt for the remainder of his time in the British army. In 1774, he resigned his commission and moved to Lancaster, Pennsylvania and practiced medicine. There he met Katherine Ewing and married her on March 13, 1775. The couple would have four children, three daughters and a son. Only one of the daughters and the son would survive to adulthood.

In April 1775 Hand had sided with the American cause against England and volunteered for service in the Continental Army. He was commissioned as a Lt. Colonel on the 1st Pennsylvania Regiment of Riflemen, made up of mostly Scots-Irish. He was second in command to Colonel William Thompson from County Meath, which is just north of Dublin. Their first assignment was to support the Continental Army's siege of Boston. They were renamed the 1st Continental Regiment, and after the siege, in March 1776 they were sent to reinforce American troops in Canada. When Colonel Thompson was captured during an attack in Quebec, Hand assumed command. After they withdrew from Canada, the regiment rejoined the Continental Army in New York.

There the regiment was involved in the Battle of Long Island in August 1776. In danger of being destroyed, Washington ordered an evacuation of the army to Manhattan. Hand and his Pennsylvania riflemen made up the rear guard and delayed the British until the rest of the army was safe across the East River in Manhattan.

Hand's regiment made up the rear guard all during the army's retreat across New Jersey to Pennsylvania. Next Hand and his Pennsylvania riflemen took part in the Battles of Trenton in December 1776 and Princeton in January 1777. Hand's men played a significant role in Trenton on

The grave of Edward Hand

Edward Hand's home, Rock Ford Plantation

January 2 that led to Washington's victory in Princeton on January 3. Impressed by Hand's consistently fine conduct and his demonstrating tactical and administrative abilities, Washington prevailed on Congress to appoint Hand Brigadier General on April 1, 1777.

Ironically he was then assigned to Fort Pitt where he improved the effectiveness of the local militia and secured the neutrality of the Delaware and Shawnee Indians.

In 1780, he was recalled from the west and given command of a brigade of light infantry in Lafayette's division. In that capacity, he sat on the court-martial that condemned Major John André to death for spying.

In 1781, Washington appointed Hand as the Adjutant General serving directly under him. He reorganized the army despite scant supplies. He also worked closely with Washington at Mt. Vernon and Williamsburg during the planning for the Siege and Battle of Yorktown which led to the surrender of the British Army in October of 1781.

At the end of the war, Hand resigned his commission from the army but not before he received a promotion to Major General in September 1783 in recognition of his long and distinguished service. He resigned in November 1783 and returned to practice medicine in Lancaster. He purchased several hundred acres of land and built a mansion he named "Rock Ford Plantation."

On November 12, 1783, the Pennsylvania legislature elected Hand to a seat in the Continental Congress. The following year Hand received a letter from Washington expressing his appreciation for the "great zeal, attention and ability manifested by you, in conducting the business of your Department, and how happy I should be in opportunities of demonstrating my sincere regard and esteem for you."

Hand served in the Pennsylvania assembly from 1785-1786 and in 1790 was chosen as a delegate to the Pennsylvania Constitutional Convention.

On September 4, 1802, Edward Hand died at his home in Lancaster. There are some reports about the cause of his death including stroke, typhoid, dysentery, pneumonia, and cholera. He is buried in St. James Episcopal Church Cemetery in Lancaster. His estate Rock Ford is a historic site and open to the public.

Joseph Hewes
(1730–1779)

First Secretary of Naval Affairs

Buried at Christ Church Burial Ground,
Philadelphia, Pennsylvania.

Continental Association • Declaration of Independence

This founder was born in New Jersey but made his mark representing the state of North Carolina. He was raised by his Quaker parents. He attended Princeton College. He then decided to go into business and moved to Philadelphia to serve as an apprentice to the successful merchant and importer Joseph Ogden. He learned enough to become a very successful merchant on his own. Already an established businessman by the age of thirty, he relocated to North Carolina. It was in his adopted state that he made a name for himself politically when he was elected to the first Continental Congress in 1774. He was still in Congress when that body declared American independence and he proudly signed the document authored by Thomas Jefferson. He is also credited with playing a leading role in the creation of the Continental Navy and many consider him the first Secretary of the Navy. His name was Joseph Hewes.

Hewes was born on January 23, 1730, in Kingston, New Jersey. There is no dispute as to the fact that he attended Princeton College. What is in dispute is whether or not he graduated. Diploma or not, he was determined to make his way in the world of business. He worked

Joseph Hewes

initially as an apprentice in Philadelphia before establishing his own successful business. In 1760 at the age of thirty, he moved to Edenton, North Carolina which was a growing seaport on the Albemarle Sound. He successfully built a thriving business there as well but, while his professional life produced prosperity, his personal life produced heartbreak. Hewes was engaged to be married to the love of his life, Isabella Johnston, who died just days before their planned wedding. He would never marry.

Hewes was active in North Carolina's political affairs and was elected to the state legislature just three years after he settled there. Though he was an advocate for the rights of the colonies, he did not hold the view that separation from the mother country was best for America. It was a position he would champion up to the day Congress passed the motion declaring America's independence.

In 1774, North Carolina elected Hewes to the First Continental Congress. As a member of Congress, he supported measures that would harm his business interests. He strongly supported and worked to establish a nonimportation association. Since much of his own business dealings involved British imports, this action cost him dearly from a financial standpoint. But money was not all this patriot sacrificed for his country.

In 1775, the Quakers held a convention which denounced the Congress of which Hewes was a member. They announced that they opposed both war and the committees of Congress formed to aid in the American effort. Hewes responded by ending his affiliation with the Quakers siding with his nation against the religious beliefs of his parents.

Hewes was noted for being a hard and tireless worker in Congress. It appears that he applied the same energy, resolve, and determination he had used to build his business in his role as a representative of his state. Absenteeism was a major problem in Congress. By the fall of 1775, often more than 30% of the delegates were missing when the delegates were called to order. Hewes seldom missed even a committee meeting. In the momentous month of July 1776, he described his work as "too severe" noting that he sometimes attended meetings for eleven to twelve hours at a stretch "without eating or drinking." His health suffered but he refused to lessen his workload writing that he "obstinately persisted in doing my duty to the best of my judgment and abilities, and attended Congress the whole time, one day excepted."

As the mood in Congress shifted toward declaring independence, Hewes remained convinced that the colonies could achieve their objectives without separating from England. Though he still hoped for reconciliation with the mother country, he put his ships at the nation's disposal. He also used his influence to push hard to get a navy commander's assignment for a friend of his by the name of John Paul Jones. Hewes worked on a committee to rig the first navy ship and served as Secretary of the Naval Affairs Committee. Though he is in competition for the title with his friend Jones, many believe that it is Hewes who deserves to be called the "Father of the Navy."

When Richard Henry Lee introduced his resolution to declare independence in June of 1776, Hewes still felt that the action was premature.

It was through the efforts of John Adams that Hewes was finally convinced to vote for independence. Adams would later recall "the unanimity of the States finally depended upon the vote of Joseph Hewes, and was finally determined by him." As for Hewes himself, after the resolution was adopted he lifted both hands and called out, "It is done! And I will abide by it."

In 1779, Hewes was still hard at work in Congress. He grew ill, probably as a result of overwork and undernourishment. Keeping his shoulder to the plow, he wrote, "My country is entitled to my services, and I shall not shrink from her cause, even though it should cost me my life." It did. Too ill to travel home to North Carolina, he died on October 10, 1779, at the age of 49. He was laid to rest in the Christ Church Burial Ground and his fellow congressmen wore a black crape around their arms for a month in his memory.

In 1894, an effort was made to move Hewes' remains back to North Carolina. On May 24th of that year, the *Wilmington Messenger* reported that his grave was lost. The paper noted that Hewes had been buried in the

The grave of Joseph Hewes

cemetery of Christ Episcopal Church in Philadelphia but that a "patient search failed to find either the grave or any record of it on the archives of the church." In 2003, the Christ Church Preservation Society published a small book written by Jean K. Wolf titled *Lives of the Silent Stones in the Christ Church Burial Ground.* In it, the author explains that the cemetery contains a donated commemorative plaque honoring Hewes because "the 1864 inscription book lists no grave marker for Joseph Hewes." Thus the burial site of this patriot and significant founder is unmarked.

Michael Hillegas
(1729–1804)

The First Treasurer

Buried at Christ Church Burial Ground,
Philadelphia, Pennsylvania.

———•◦•———

1st Treasurer of U.S.A.

Michael Hillegas, of Huguenot descent, though not an elected member of the Continental Congress, served as the first treasurer of the United States along with George Clymer. They worked together to create a stable financial foundation for the young nation. He later served as the sole Treasurer of the United States and Treasurer for the state of Pennsylvania.

⋘⋙•◦•⋘⋙

Born in Philadelphia, Pennsylvania on April 22, 1729, Michael Hillegas was the son of George Michael Hillegas (1696-1749) and his wife Margaret (née Schiebenstock). The elder Hillegas was originally from Alsace but moved to the Palatinate to escape religious persecution. A merchant by trade, he emigrated to Pennsylvania, settling in Philadelphia, where he became a naturalized citizen and leader in the German community. The elder Hillegas amassed real estate functioning as a potter, innkeeper, and storekeeper. He passed away in 1749 and is buried at Christ Church. His wife passed in 1770 and is buried next to him.

Michael Hillegas was well-educated thanks to his father's social standing. He followed in his father's footsteps as a businessman. According to *The Magazine of History* (1907), "Mr. Hillegas was rated among the wealthiest citizens of Philadelphia in pre-Revolutionary times. He was

Michael Hillegas

the owner of the largest sugar refinery in the city, was interested in the manufacture of iron, was a merchant whose services were sought by the State and city governments, and prominent in the best society of the city." On May 10, 1753, he married Henrietta Boude at Christ Church. The couple had ten children.

Before age 35, in 1762, Hillegas was appointed as one of the commissioners to recommend a site for a fort to defend Philadelphia. This later became Fort Mifflin. In 1763 or 1765 (sources vary), he was elected to a seat in the Pennsylvania Provincial Assembly which he held until 1775.

Throughout his experience with the Pennsylvania Assembly, he became adept at accounting and learned how to manage government spending. As the royal government began to collapse in 1774, Hillegas was named to the Committees of Observation and Safety to oversee the embargos demanded by the Continental Association. In 1775, he was appointed as a member of the Pennsylvania Council of Safety led by Benjamin Franklin, and, on June 30 of that year, was named its Treasurer.

Hillegas was well-known to those in the colonies who were planning the Revolution. John Adams wrote in his diary on October 28, 1775:

The Congress and the Assembly of this Province [Pennsylvania] were invited to make an excursion, upon [the] Delaware River, in the new row gallies built by the Committee of Safety of this Colony. About ten in the morning, we all embarked. The names of the gallies are the *Washington*, the *Effingham*, the *Franklin*, the *Dickinson*, the *Otter*, the *Bull Dog*, and one more whose name I have forgotten. We passed down the river, by Gloucester, where the *vaisseaux de frise* are. These are frames of timber, to be filled with stones, and sunk in three rows in the channel. I went in the *Bull Dog*, Captain Alexander, commander, Mr. Hillegas, Mr. Owen Biddle, and Mr. [David] Rittenhouse, and Captain Faulkner were with me. Hillegas is one of our continental treasurers; is a great musician; talks perpetually of the forte and piano, of Handel, etc., and songs and tunes. He plays upon the fiddle.

On July 29, 1775, the Continental Congress voted Michael Hillegas and George Clymer as co-treasurers of the United Colonies. Their initial task was to manage the distribution and circulation of over three million dollars in continental currency.

On May 30, 1776, Hillegas was named the Treasurer for the Province of Pennsylvania, a position he held even after Pennsylvania declared its statehood.

During the summer of 1776, Clymer signed the Declaration of Independence. Because Hillegas was an editor of the document, he did not sign, though he was present. The following month, upon Clymer's resignation as Treasurer, Hillegas became the sole Treasurer of the United States, a position he held until 1789.

In the *Dictionary of American Biography*, historian John Frederick wrote, "During the Revolution, he [Hillegas] contributed a large part of his fortune, by gift or loan, to the support of the army, and in 1781 he was one of the first subscribers to the Bank of North America. By direction of the Pennsylvania General Assembly he compiled and published, in 1782, Volume I of [the] Journals of the House of Representatives of the Commonwealth of Pennsylvania, covering the period between November 28, 1776, and October 2, 1781. This task stimulated his interest in the preservation of historical material. In a letter of August 20, 1781, to the governor of New Hampshire, he suggested 'the propriety of each legislature in the Union adopting measures similar to those taken by this state for the above purpose.'" Hillegas was also one of the founders of the Bank of Pennsylvania in 1780.

As the new constitution was being ratified, Hillegas lobbied George Washington to continue in his duties. In a letter to Washington on September 5, 1789, Hillegas wrote:

> From Michael Hillegas
> New York Septr 5. 1789
>
> Sir.
> As the time for making appointments under the Treasury Law draws near, I beg leave to Request Your Excellency's remembrance of the present Treasurer, who has the honor to be with the greatest Respect Your Excellency's most Obedt humble Servt
>
> M. Hillegas

On September 11, 1789, under the new United States Constitution, Alexander Hamilton was sworn in as the first Secretary of the Treasury, and Michael Hillegas resigned from his position.

His national duties behind him, Hillegas retired to Philadelphia affairs where he continued to function as an alderman and an early member of the American Philosophical Society until his death in 1804. He was laid to rest at Christ Church Burial Ground in Philadelphia, a few yards from Benjamin Franklin.

Relatives of Hillegas later petitioned to have his portrait appear on the ten-dollar gold certificate. These notes bearing his likeness were issued from 1907 to 1922.

Said an unnamed historian in *The Magazine of History* (1907):

> That Michael Hillegas' fame should have been obscured
> so long is explainable only on the ground that he was of

German-French descent, and that the principal historians of the day were Quakers who preferred to have it appear that the followers of William Penn were the principal actors in the history of Philadelphia. That this is the explanation is indicated by the president of a Quaker college who recently wrote a history of Pennsylvania, and who explained his omission of all reference to Mr. Hillegas by saying it was an "oversight," adding that he found Mr. Hillegas' name "hundreds of times" in his investigations. Another reason may be that while the descendants of Robert Morris and Samuel Meredith, other claimants to the title of first treasurer, have been busy inducting States to erect monuments to their forebears, there have been no such active descendants of Mr. Hillegas, there being no lineal stock bearing his name.

The grave of Micahel Hillegas

Francis Hopkinson
(1737–1791)

The Patriot Renaissance Man

Buried at Christ Church Burial Ground,
Philadelphia, Pennsylvania.

Declaration of Independence

In 1924 a Pennsylvanian historian wrote that this founder was a poet and a scientist. As it turns out, that description is an understatement. He was also a mathematician, mechanic, musician, composer, inventor of musical instruments, a lawyer by profession, and a signer of the Declaration of Independence. He was a man who could indeed be termed a Jack of many arts and perhaps a master of some. His name was Francis Hopkinson.

Hopkinson was born in Philadelphia on September 21, 1737. His father, Thomas Hopkinson, was a close friend of Benjamin Franklin. The duo was so close that they co-founded the University of Pennsylvania. It is not surprising that Hopkinson himself was a member of the first class educated by the college his father helped establish. He graduated in 1757 and received a master's degree in 1760.

After college Hopkinson studied law under Benjamin Chew, who was the Attorney General of the province. He was admitted to the bar in 1761 and was considered an able lawyer. However, his many interests encroached on both his ability and time to practice law. In the same year, he was admitted to the bar he was called upon to perform his initial act of public service. He served as secretary to a conference held on the banks of the Lehigh

Francis Hopkinson

River between the Indians of that area and Governor James Hamilton. He wrote a poem titled "The Treaty" that was inspired by this experience.

In 1766 he sailed for Europe where he lived for approximately a year in Ireland and England. When he returned to America, he resumed his law practice and opened a dry goods business in Philadelphia. In 1768 he married a Jersey girl, Ann Borden, and the couple would produce five children including the jurist and statesman Joseph Hopkinson who wrote the lyrics to "Hail Columbia." That song was recognized by many as the de facto national anthem of the United States until the country adopted "The Star-Spangled Banner" when that piece was recognized as the official anthem by Congress in 1931.

After his marriage, Hopkinson moved to Bordentown, New Jersey. When he first entered the practice of law, Hopkinson took legal positions supporting the crown. However, as time passed, he grew to favor American independence, and he resigned from the English colonial government positions. In June of 1776, he was elected to represent New Jersey in the

Second Continental Congress. As a member of Congress, he made enough of an impression on John Adams that the future president conveyed his thoughts on Hopkinson in a letter to his wife, Abigail. Adams wrote, "I met Mr. Francis Hopkinson, late a mandamus councilor of New Jersey, now a member of Continental Congress, who was liberally educated and is now a painter and a poet. I have a curiosity to delve a little deeper into the bosom of this curious gentleman, and may possibly give you more particulars concerning him. He is one of your pretty, little, curious, ingenious men. His head is no bigger than a large apple. I have not met with anything in natural history more amusing and entertaining than his personal appearance, yet he is genteel and well-bred and very social." There is little doubt that Adams was pleased when Hopkinson voted in favor of independence and subsequently signed the document declaring the same.

As a member of Congress, Hopkinson served as the Treasurer of Loans in the young nation's Treasury Department. He also wrote patriotic songs and drew caricatures of other members of Congress. One of the songs he composed titled "The Battle of the Kegs" became the best known of all ballads written during the Revolutionary period. He also worked on designing seals for various agencies of the government and was a member of the committee given the job of designing the Great Seal of the United States.

In 1779 Hopkinson was appointed to the position of Judge of the Admiralty for Pennsylvania. He served in this position until 1789. In that same year, President Washington made him the United States District Judge for Pennsylvania; a position he would hold until his death.

Hopkinson also used his talents to support the ratification of the Constitution. In 1787 he wrote the poem and allegorical essay "The New Roof" to aid in the effort to have the states accept the new form of government that the Constitutional Convention had proposed. In the work, he describes architects who had discovered a weakness in a mansion house composed of thirteen rafters in need of repair. The rafters represented the original colonies. His work ends with the words, "Figure to yourselves, my good fellows, a man with a cow and a horse - oh the battlements, the battlements, they will fall upon his cow, they will fall upon his horse and wound them, and the poor man will perish with hunger. The architects of the new structure (Constitution) would save both the building and the man's possessions."

The grave of Francis Hopkinson

In 1927 Dr. G. E. Hastings, a professor of English at the University of Arkansas, asserted that Hopkinson and not Betsy Ross was the actual designer of the first American flag. Hastings based his claim on his examination of documents in the archives of the Congressional Library. There he found that Hopkinson had submitted a bill to Congress that requested payment for the work he had done designing the flag. His asking price was "a Quarter cask of the Public Wine." Congress responded by saying that as an employee of the Treasury, his pay had covered any work he had done. While he was never paid, Hastings and other historians have correctly concluded that Hopkinson is the only person in the minutes of the Continental Congress credited with having designed a United States flag.

According to Doctor Benjamin Rush, Hopkinson was "seized with an apoplectic fit" on the morning of May 9, 1791. He died shortly after that and was laid to rest in Philadelphia's Christ Church Burial Ground. As a result of rumors that he wasn't buried in that cemetery, remains were exhumed in the 1930s and inspected by a University of Pennsylvania anatomist. The conclusion was that the remains were Hopkinson's. As his tombstone had deteriorated over the years, when he was reburied, a new memorial was added to the site. Among the credits now listed on the bronze plaque that rests above him is "Designer of the American Flag."

Charles Humphreys
(1717–1786)

A Patriot Who Followed His Conscience

Buried at Old Haverford Friends Meeting House Cemetery,
Havertown, Pennsylvania.

————•◆•————

Continental Association

This founder was one of the older members of the Continental Congress.
A miller by trade he did not begin his political career until he was 50 years
of age. As a member of Congress, he signed the Continental Association.
He voted against the Declaration of Independence and refused to sign
the document. The decision to vote against independence led to his resignation from Congress soon after independence was declared. Though
he did not take part in the Revolution, his sympathies were with the
Americans, and he criticized what he saw as oppression by the British
government. His name was Charles Humphreys.

————◆◆◆————

Humphreys was born at his family estate which was located about
seven miles northwest of Philadelphia in the village of Haverford on
September 19, 1714. His father was a Welsh immigrant who arrived
in the colonies in 1682 and went into business as a miller, one who
mills grains like wheat, for example. Charles Humphreys attended local
schools, but there is no evidence that he received any advanced school-
ing. After completing his preparatory studies, he took up his father's
profession.

Charles Humphreys

Based on information in *The Pennsylvania Magazine Of History And Biography*, Humphreys "was held in high regard for his talents, his integrity in private and public life, his hospitality and courteous and dignified manners." Perhaps based on this sterling reputation in1764 the British government appointed him to a seat in the Pennsylvania Provincial Congress. Humphreys would serve in that body for a full decade. Though the organization served as little more than a rubber stamp for decisions made by the British Parliament, as a result of his efforts his status as a local statesman continued to flourish.

In 1774 Humphreys was elected to the Continental Congress. That same year in response to the British Parliament passing the Coercive Acts restructuring the administration of the colonies and specifically punishing Massachusetts for the Boston Tea Party, Congress adopted the Continental Association. The Association was a system designed to implement a trade boycott aimed at the banning the importing and consumption of any goods from England, Ireland and the British West Indies. The Association avoided blaming the king for the problems instead pointing the finger at Parliament and lower British officials for a "ruinous system of colony administration." Humphreys was among the delegates that signed the Continental Association.

There is little doubt that the toughest question Humphreys wrestled with as a member of Congress was that of American independence. Based on his religious beliefs, Humphreys, a Quaker, opposed going to war. But, he was well aware, as pointed out in 1923 by the lawyer and scholar Hampton L. Carson in the *Philadelphia Inquirer*, that the charter of William Penn included a provision that allowed the Crown to tax the colonists without their consent. In the end, his religious beliefs, more than anything else, led him to vote against American independence and refuse to sign the document authored by Jefferson once it was passed. Humphreys, much like John Dickinson, was a patriot who did not believe that separation from the mother country was the right course to pursue.

After the Declaration was adopted, Humphreys left Congress. Little is known about his later life. Mr. Carson mentioned earlier wrote that Humphreys contributed his share to the patriot cause. The Humphreys family continued to work for the country after the Revolution. For example, his nephew Joshua Humphreys was a shipbuilder and naval architect who was responsible for the construction of the original six frigates

The grave of Charles Humphreys

of the United States Navy. These ships included the USS *Constellation* and the USS *Constitution*.

Charles Humphreys died on March 11, 1786, at his estate near Philadelphia. He was laid to rest in the Old Haverford Friends Meeting House Cemetery. After his death, a newspaper said of him, "From a very early period of his life distinguished by integrity and sound understanding, his country fixed on him to fill those public stations with which she rewards the upright and the just. In the General Assembly - in Congress, he was known to be liberal and impartial. In private life open, hospitable, and generous - and in death, serene and unruffled - so that we may safely say he died sincerely lamented by friends, and much respected even by his enemies."

Jared Ingersoll
(1749–1822)

Pennsylvania Attorney General

Buried at Old Pine Street Presbyterian Church Cemetery,
Philadelphia, Pennsylvania.

———•◦•———

U.S. Constitution

This founder's father was a British colonial official and later a loyalist during the American Revolution. Though he initially shared his father's views, he would evolve and fully commit to the cause of American independence. He studied the law and became a leading Philadelphia attorney. He was elected to and served in the Continental Congress in 1780-81. In 1787, he was one of the delegates representing Pennsylvania at the Constitutional Convention and he signed the document that was created by that gathering. He would later serve as the Attorney General of Pennsylvania, the United States District Attorney for Pennsylvania, and the presiding judge of the Philadelphia District Court. In 1812, he was the Federalist candidate for the office of Vice President. His name was Jared Ingersoll.

———•◦•———

Ingersoll was born on November 7, 1749, in New Haven, Connecticut. He received a solid education and graduated from Yale in 1766. He then studied law in Philadelphia and was admitted to the Pennsylvania bar in 1773. His father was a British colonial agent who had actually served in the position of Stamp Master in Connecticut after the Stamp Act was

Jared Ingersoll

imposed on the colonies in 1765. After assuming that position, the elder Ingersoll became one of the most hated men in his colony. The Sons of Liberty hung his effigy on August 21 of the same year he took that office.

In 1773, with revolutionary passions running high, Ingersoll, heeding his father's advice, sailed to London to continue his study of law and travel throughout Europe. During this time, he spent 18 months in Paris where he was welcomed by Benjamin Franklin who was a friend of the family. One of the reasons he left England for France was the news that the colonies had declared their independence. Shortly after the colonies' declaration, Ingersoll broke with his family's views and made a personal commitment to the patriot cause. He didn't view remaining in England as an option. He returned to America in 1778, arriving in Philadelphia where, with the help of friends, not the least being Joseph Reed the president of the state, he established a successful law practice.

In 1780-81 he was elected to and served in the Continental Congress. After the Revolution, Ingersoll became convinced that the Articles of Confederation had to be amended if the union was to survive. He was chosen as one of Pennsylvania's representatives to the 1787 Constitutional Convention. He entered the convention believing that the Articles merely needed to be amended to render them effective. He was a regular though silent representative at the gathering in Philadelphia. He spoke but once at the convention and left behind no written recollections of the assembly except his signature on the Constitution itself. He did later say that he did not believe his signing of the document should be regarded as a pledge to support it in every particular describing it as "a recommendation of what, all things considered, was the most eligible." He would get the opportunity to argue several cases before the United States Supreme

The grave of Jared Ingersoll

Court that aided in ironing out some of the finer points regarding constitutional law.

After the Constitution was ratified, Ingersoll devoted his energies to service to the city of Philadelphia as a judge and to his state as the Attorney General. He remained a Federalist who ardently opposed the election of Thomas Jefferson in 1800. In 1812, he became the candidate for Vice President on the Federalist ticket headed by DeWitt Clinton. The Federalists failed in their attempt to defeat President James Madison, losing the electoral vote by a 128 to 89 margin. Ingersoll failed to deliver the crucial electoral votes of his home state.

Ingersoll passed away at the age of 72, just a week before his 73rd birthday, on October 31, 1822, in Philadelphia. He was laid to rest in the Old Pine Street Presbyterian Church Cemetery located in that city. It was said of Ingersoll that he had one conviction that stood out, it being that patriots should serve for the honor of one thing, for the glory of their country, and never just as a means of livelihood or selfish prestige.

William Jackson
(1759–1828)

Secretary of the Constitutional Convention

Buried at Christ Church Burial Ground,
Philadelphia, Pennsylvania.

————•◦•————

U.S. Constitution • Military

William Jackson was an officer in the Continental Army who served with distinction during the American Revolution. He leveraged his connections, especially with George Washington, to become the secretary of the United States Constitutional Convention where he was the 40th person to affix his signature. Jackson also served President George Washington as one of his secretaries during his administration.

————•◦•————

William Jackson was born March 9, 1759, in the county of Cumberland, England, located in the northern part of the country near Scotland. He was just a boy when his parents passed away. Now an orphan, neighbors arranged for his emigration to Charleston, South Carolina soon after. There he was raised by a family friend, Owen Roberts, who was a prominent merchant and militia commander. Roberts, a veteran of the French and Indian War, involved the young man in many of the militia's activities.

When the Revolutionary War began in 1775, Roberts was an ardent patriot and brought his teenaged charge along with him. By May of 1776, just seventeen years of age, Jackson was commissioned as a

William Jackson

second lieutenant in the 1st South Carolina Regiment led by Colonel Christopher Gadsden.

The following month, in June 1776, Jackson saw his first action defending against British General Clinton's assault on Fort Sullivan, since renamed Fort Moultrie, at the entrance to Charleston harbor. He then spent most of the next year garrisoned in Charleston until, under Major General Robert Howe, he was part of the failed attempt to take St. Augustine, Florida, from the British. While many were struck down by disease, Jackson survived and returned to South Carolina in 1778.

After his return, Congress replaced Howe with Major General Benjamin Lincoln. Charles Cotesworth Pinckney convinced Lincoln he, a northerner from Massachusetts, could use a local aide to assist him with his southern troops. Jackson was tapped for the position and promoted to major. Jackson then served with Lincoln in the skirmishes that followed the loss of Savannah, including the battle of Stono Ferry in June 1779, where his guardian Owen Roberts was killed, and the American counteroffensive at Savannah in conjunction with comte d'Estaing's French forces. Jackson experienced defeat in both instances, and the allies retreated from Savannah, blaming each other for the failure.

Worse yet, in 1780, General Clinton turned his focus from Savannah to Charleston and was this time successful. Lincoln was forced to surrender after a lengthy siege of forty-two days. Jackson and 5,000 rebels were captured and taken prisoner. Jackson was taken to Philadelphia on parole and held there by the British until he, Lincoln, and others were exchanged.

Jackson was next assigned as secretary to South Carolinian Lieutenant Colonel John Laurens, the son of Henry Laurens, who was George Washington's aide thanks to Lincoln's recommendation. In 1781 this put Jackson on John Barry's boat with Laurens on the mission to France to negotiate for war supplies. Jackson's mastery of French was highly valued. For six weeks they dealt with Minister of Foreign Affairs comte de Vergennes at Versaille to no avail. Finally, direct contact was made with the King of France and Washington's request handed to him. The King then loaned the requested funds, most of which was spent on supplies.

Laurens returned to America with three ships full of materiel while Jackson went to Holland where John Adams had contracted for a fourth ship. This, however, never came to pass. Either Adams was deceived, or the ship was sunk. Despite being chased by the British navy, Laurens arrived in Boston in September. Jackson finally returned in February 1782.

Next, Jackson served as the assistant secretary of war under Benjamin Lincoln and helped settle the Pennsylvania Mutiny of 1783. Hundreds of Pennsylvania soldiers demanded to be paid for their services during the Revolution and took over Congress in Philadelphia. Eventually, the revolt was put down, but Congress moved to New Jersey and then New York for a time.

In October 1783, with the demobilization of the Continental Army complete, Jackson resigned his office and his commission to become Robert Morris's agent in England for several months. His prospects had changed since Owen Roberts was killed in 1779 and he needed to earn a living. When he returned in 1784, Jackson studied law in Philadelphia with William Lewis.

Before concluding his law studies, getting wind of the upcoming Constitutional Convention in Philadelphia, Jackson wrote to Washington to apply for the post as secretary. On May 25, 1787, Alexander Hamilton nominated Jackson. He won out over Benjamin Franklin's grandson, William Temple Franklin, who had been his grandfather's secretary during the negotiations of the Treaty of Paris.

As convention secretary, Jackson was sworn to secrecy regarding the proceedings, kept the official minutes, and destroyed all records except for the official journal after the final draft of the Constitution was signed. There had been a debate about the destruction of the journals which contained many proposals and counterproposals not adopted. Said Rufus King of Massachusetts, "If suffered to be made public a bad use would be made of them." Two suggestions were made regarding them: destroy them or deposit them into the custody of the president, George Washington, "until Congress, if ever formed under the Constitution" would give him further instructions. It was decided to do the latter, and the records remained with Washington until December 1796 when he gave them to the Department of State. Congress prohibited publication of the journals until 1818 when John Quincy Adams, the Secretary of State, discovered the decaying state of the papers.

While not a voting member of the Constitutional Convention, Jackson signed the document "Attest William Jackson Secretary" and thus became the fortieth signer of the U.S. Constitution, his signature authenticating the others.

Days after the signing, on September 20, 1787, Jackson was sent to the Congress assembled in New York City with a copy of the Constitution and read it aloud.

Jackson was admitted to the Pennsylvania Bar in 1788 but had to wait two years to practice before the Pennsylvania Supreme Court, as was customary. In the meantime, he applied to be the secretary to the United States Senate but did not get the position; however, George Washington brought him on as his secretary while he was president.

The grave of William Jackson

Jackson resigned in 1791 to start his law practice, despite being offered the post of Adjutant General of the Army, and worked with Henry Knox, the Secretary of War, and William Bingham who were selling off a large land grant in Maine they had acquired. Jackson went to England and France to sell the land on commission.

Jackson returned to the United States in the summer of 1795 and married Elizabeth Willing, the sister of Mrs. Bingham, that November. The ladies were the daughters of Thomas Willing, the Philadelphia financier. George and Martha Washington, Robert and Mary Morris, Alexander Hamilton, and Benjamin Lincoln were among those who attended the wedding.

The Jacksons produced four children. A son William married Martha James but had no children. There were also three daughters: Mary (married Rigal), Ann (married Willing), and Caroline.

In January 1796, during his final months in office, Washington appointed Jackson Collector for the Port of Philadelphia responsible for collecting customs tariffs.

Due to his Federalist associations, Jackson was dismissed by President Thomas Jefferson in 1801 despite the fact Jefferson had been a guest at Jackson's nuptials. Jackson then started the *Political and Commerical Register*, a Federalist newspaper based in Philadelphia. Jackson was the editor until 1815.

Jackson also returned to the law, and in one of his last significant cases, he represented Continental Army veterans who were petitioning for pensions. Jackson had succeeded Henry Knox as secretary-general of the Society of the Cincinnati in 1799, a post he held until his death.

In 1824, Jackson welcomed his old friend and ally General Lafayette to Philadelphia during his tour of America.

Jackson passed away at the age of 69 on December 18, 1828, in Philadelphia. He was buried at Christ Church Burial Ground in Philadelphia near his father-in-law. His wife lived another 30 years, passing on August 5, 1858.

Philip Livingston
(1716 – 1778)

Died in York

Buried at Prospect Hill Cemetery,
York, Pennsylvania.

Continental Association • Declaration of Independence

Philip Livingston opposed violence and once said that independence was "a vain shallow and ridiculous project" and warned that America would collapse if separated from England.

On his first trip out of Massachusetts, John Adams was on his way to Philadelphia to serve as a member of the Continental Congress. On a stop in New York, he was able to arrange meetings with some of New York's representatives that would serve in Congress with him. Among these was Philip Livingston. Adams found that Livingston not only opposed revolution but that he distrusted New Englanders. Livingston questioned Adams as to why Massachusetts had once hanged Quakers and used the incident to argue that a revolution would only result in the colonies fighting each other. Adams later said that it was impossible to reason with Livingston. However, the behavior of the British government eventually turned the New Yorker into an ardent patriot and an active promoter of efforts to raise and fund troops for the war.

Livingston was born on January 15, 1716, in Albany, New York into a prosperous family. His father Robert Livingston had emigrated

Philip Livingston

to America from Scotland in 1673. He settled in Albany and quickly established himself in the fur trade. In 1687 the English Royal Governor granted him ownership of a tract of land consisting of 160,000 acres on the east bank of the Hudson River. The land became known as the "Manor of Livingston" and remains in the family to the present day.

Robert saw to it that young Philip was tutored at home and then attended and graduated from Yale University in 1737. After marrying Christina Broeck, the daughter of the mayor of Albany, the couple settled in New York City where he became a very successful merchant and took an active part in civic affairs. His accomplishments during this time included pushing for the founding of Kings College (known today as Columbia University), the establishment of a Professorship of Divinity at Yale, the building of the first meeting house for the Methodist Society in America, and providing aid to organize the New York Public Library. In 1754 he was elected an alderman in the City, his first venture into public life. He would continue to be elected alderman for nine consecutive years. His success in these elections suggests that he was perceived as an effective representative by those who were able to cast ballots. In 1758 he was also elected to the Colonial Legislature and would urge moderation in dealings with England.

In 1765 he attended the Stamp Act Congress which produced the first formal protest to the Crown. In July 1775, he signed the Olive Branch Petition, a final attempt to achieve an understanding with the Crown. The petition appealed directly to King George III to cease hostilities and restore harmony. The King refused to respond to the plea and proclaimed the Colonies to be in a state of rebellion. Livingston was elected to the First and Second Continental Congress and during this time he changed his mind and supported the Revolution and signed the Declaration of Independence in 1776. He accepted independence reluctantly, dreading the social upheaval.

In September 1775, he was one of nine men appointed to the Secret Committee—later known as the Committee on Commerce—charged

The grave of Philip Livingston

with arranging the importation of arms and gunpowder for the patriot forces. He remained a member throughout his time in Congress and spent a large part of his own money to purchase supplies for the army. When the British army captured New York City, they seized his two houses forcing his family to flee to Kingston. They used his Duke Street home as a barracks and his Brooklyn Heights residence as a Royal Navy Hospital.

Unfortunately, Livingston did not live to see the American victory. He was re-elected to Congress in October 1777. During this particularly critical and gloomy period in the Revolution, Congress was forced to meet in York, Pennsylvania because the British had seized Philadelphia. Livingston's health was precarious, as he was diagnosed with dropsy in the chest (today it would be called congestive heart failure) with no rational prospect of recovery or improvement. Yet his love of his country was unwavering, and so he did not hesitate to give up the comforts of home and family.

With his health declining, he made the trip to York after bidding his friends and family a final farewell. He believed he would never return. He proved to be correct; on June 12, 1778, Philip Livingston died. He was sixty-two years old. The entire Congress attended his funeral and declared a mourning period of a month. He was first buried in a churchyard at the German Reformed Church on West Market Street in York but later moved to Prospect Hill Cemetery in York. In 2005, Descendants of the Signers of the Declaration of Independence honored him by attaching a plaque to his tombstone identifying him as a Signer of the Declaration. A number of the direct descendants took part in the dedication ceremony.

William Maclay
(1737–1804)

The First Democrat

Buried at Paxton Presbyterian Churchyard,
Harrisburg, Pennsylvania.

—— • • • ——

Military • United States Senator

This founder fought as a soldier in both the French and Indian War and the American Revolution. In the latter conflict, he participated in the Battles of Trenton and Princeton. He wed Mary McClure Harris who was the daughter of John Harris who founded the city of Harrisburg. He served as the clerk of courts for Northumberland County and as a surveyor laid out the town of Sunbury. After the Constitution was ratified, he was one of Pennsylvania's first two men elected to represent his state in the United States Senate. As a Senator, he opposed any movement toward the monarchical tendencies of the Senate a position that often put him at odds with Vice President John Adams and Alexander Hamilton. He fiercely opposed Hamilton's plan to get the young country on solid financial footing. His fervent embrace of Jeffersonian Republicanism earned him the title of the earliest Democrat. His name was William Maclay.

—— • • • ——

Maclay was born on July 20, 1737. His parents sent him to the classical school run by the Reverend John Blair, and he proved to be an industrious student. He decided to study law, and in 1760 he was admitted to the York County Bar. During this period he served as a lieutenant in the

William Maclay

French and Indian War. He distinguished himself as both a soldier and a leader in this conflict. It was as a direct result of his military service that his practice of the law was curtailed. Much of his time and energy went into surveying lands that had been allocated to officers who served in the war. It was this experience that led to his role in surveying Sunbury, a town where he lived for many years, with his wife, Mary McClure Harris. Between 1770 and 1787 the couple would produce eleven children eight of which survived infancy.

When the American Revolution began, Maclay was working for the colonial government. Despite this, he took an active part in favor of independence. In addition to serving in the Continental Army and fighting in the crucial battles of Trenton and Princeton, he worked on equipping and recruiting troops for the Continental Army.

In 1778, during the "Great Runaway" which followed the Wyoming Massacre, Maclay and his family fled Sunbury for Harris Ferry now known as Harrisburg. In letters to the president of the Executive Council he described in detail the distress felt in the area as a result of the attacks by the British Tories and their Indian allies. In 1781 he was elected to the Assembly where he served at various times as a member of the Supreme Executive Council, Judge of the Court Of Common Pleas And deputy coroner.

In 1789 he was elected as one of the first two senators representing Pennsylvania in the United States Senate. It was as a Senator in the first Congress that Maclay earned the moniker the "First Democrat." The historian Frederic A. Godcharles credited Maclay with being "the original promoter and later the actual founder of the Democratic Party." He was unafraid and unapologetic about voicing his disagreements with the Washington administration. He objected to the President being present while the Senate was conducting business. Yet the presence of America's first President did not deter him from voicing his disagreements with Washington and often with his Secretary of the Treasury Alexander Hamilton.

While serving as a senator, Maclay kept a diary that has been reprinted and titled *The Private Journal of Senator William Maclay, United States Senator, 1789-1791.* That journal is widely regarded as one of the most important political diaries in American history. It recounts his life as a member of the First Congress. He also details Senate debates, the politics of the time, and comments on his fellow members of Congress.

Maclay's diary makes one thing abundantly clear; he probably disliked Vice President John Adams more than any other member of Congress. The feeling was mutual. Adams viewed Maclay as an uncooperative troublemaker. Maclay described Adams as "a monkey just put into Breeches." The feud came back to hurt Maclay during his efforts to have the nation's capital placed in the town of Columbia, Pennsylvania which is located on the Susquehanna River. After a tie vote in the Senate on where to place the capital, Adams was in the position of casting the tie-breaking vote. The decision was on whether the nation's home would be along the Potomac or in Pennsylvania either along the Susquehanna or in Germantown. According to Maclay, Adams flattered the Virginians by praising the Potomac before making less than flattering remarks about the Susquehanna before casting his vote in favor of Germantown. Thanks to James Madison, the Senate bill failed to pass the House without amendment and as a result, was returned to the upper house where it was postponed until the next session of Congress. When the matter was finally settled, the Virginians made a deal with Alexander Hamilton which resulted in Washington, D.C. being the nation's capital. The deal also resulted in the passage of Hamilton's financial plan, which Maclay viewed as an "accursed thing which I fear future generations will hate."

Maclay was hardly a silent Senator. He often spoke during floor debates. He found himself at odds with his colleagues and in the minority on many issues. These included Senate rules, the jurisdiction of the federal judiciary, and the relationship between the legislative and executive branches. In opposing Hamilton's financial plan, he also lost respect for President Washington. He viewed Washington as being "in the hands of Hamilton the Dishclout of every dirty speculation, as his name goes to wipe away blame and silence all murmuring." As a direct result of his failure to support Hamilton's financial plan, the Pennsylvania Assembly refused to re-elect him to the Senate.

Maclay returned to Harrisburg where as a member of Jefferson's Democratic-Republican Party he lost a bid for a seat in the House of Representatives. From 1795 to 1798 he represented Dauphin County in the State House Of Representatives. As a member of this body, he supported a constitutional amendment which limited the terms of United States Senators to three years. He voted against an address expressing regret at the retirement of President Washington and introduced a resolution declaring Pennsylvania's opposition to war and with France specifically. This final act was not a popular position, and he lost a bid for re-election in 1798. He was re-elected five years later in 1803. On April 16 of the following year, he passed away in Harrisburg. He was laid to rest in Harrisburg's Paxton Presbyterian Churchyard.

At the time of his death the political party he helped found controlled the country. In looking back at his life, he may have viewed it much as he viewed his two years in the Senate. On the night he served his last day as a Senator he wrote, "As I left the hall, I gave it a look with that kind of satisfaction which a man feels on leaving a place. Where he has been ill at ease, being fully satisfied that many a culprit has served two years at the wheelbarrow—a punishment for felons—without feeling half the pain and mortification that I experienced in my honorable station." This founder may have been too hard on himself or, on the other hand, he may have just been a little ahead of his countrymen.

There is a street in Harrisburg named for Maclay, and his former home still stands alongside his beloved Susquehanna River. The Pennsylvania Bar Association are the current owners. The house contains a modern portrait of Maclay based on a miniature that was owned by one of his descendants.

The grave of William Maclay

Thomas McKean
(1735–1817)

The Simultaneous Governor of Delaware
and Chief Justice of Pennsylvania

Buried at Laurel Hill Cemetery,
Philadelphia, Pennsylvania.

———•◦•———

**Military • Declaration of Independence • President of Congress
Articles of Confederation**

This founder was known for his very brusque take-charge attitude that at times upset his fellow patriots. This may have contributed to the fact that while serving in the Stamp Act Congress, two other delegates challenged him to duels which he speedily accepted. Only the departure of one representative and the existence of cooler heads avoided the shedding of blood. His resume is lengthy and in addition to service in Congress included service in the military. He also served as Governor of Delaware and as Chief Justice of Pennsylvania at the same time. He would later attend the Pennsylvania convention that ratified the United States Constitution and serve as the Governor of that state. He also affixed his signature to both the Declaration of Independence and the Articles of Confederation. Some contend that he served as one of the first Presidents of the United States under those Articles. His name was Thomas McKean.

———◈•◈———

McKean was born on March 19, 1734, in New London Township located in Chester County, Pennsylvania. His parents were both Irish

Thomas McKean

born Ulster-Scots who came to America from Ballymoney, County Antrim, Ireland. When McKean was 16 years of age, he traveled to New Castle, Delaware to study the law under one of his cousins. By 1756 he had been admitted to the bar in both Delaware and Pennsylvania. By the mid-1760s he was serving in the Delaware General Assembly and as a judge of the Court of Common Pleas. Delaware at the time had two political factions which were commonly referred to as the "Court Party" and the "Country Party." The former party urged reconciliation with England while the latter, of which McKean was a leading member, supported American independence.

In 1765, Mckean and Caesar Rodney represented Delaware at the Stamp Act Congress. McKean was an active member of this group and along with John Rutledge and Philip Livingston served on the committee that drafted the Declaration of Rights and Grievances. Timothy Ruggles, a delegate from Massachusetts who served as president of the body, refused to sign the Memorial. Ruggles also declined to state the reasons for his objection. McKean wouldn't let the matter drop and demanded that Ruggles explain himself. The Massachusetts delegate then explained that his conscience would not permit him to address complaints to the king. McKean responded with scorn twice bellowing out the word conscience in a sarcastic manner that Ruggles viewed as an insult. He challenged McKean to a duel which was immediately accepted. Early the next morning Ruggles returned to his home state, so no duel was fought. The Massachusetts legislature officially censured Ruggles for "a neglect of duty." Ruggles wasn't the only delegate at the gathering to draw McKean's ire. Robert Ogden, a representative from New Jersey, also challenged McKean to a meeting on the field of honor. McKean accepted this invitation but cooler heads in attendance interceded, and the quarrel was settled without a shot being fired.

McKean would marry twice and father eleven children. His first wife, Mary Borden, passed away in 1773. A year later he married Sarah Armitage and moved his family to Philadelphia. Despite his Pennsylvania residence he was elected to represent Delaware in the Continental Congress. As a member of Congress, McKean is remembered for the part he played in fellow delegate Caesar Rodney's midnight ride. On July 1, 1776, McKean concluded that another delegate from Delaware, George Read, intended to vote against declaring American independence. Rodney, who like McKean favored independence, was absent from Congress due to a severe illness. Realizing that Rodney's vote would be needed McKean sent a messenger to Rodney who had returned to his home in Dover, Delaware. The message urged his fellow delegate to return to Philadelphia at once. Rodney immediately mounted a horse and began the eighty-mile trip back to Congress. As McKean later remembered in a letter to one of Rodney's nephews, he met Rodney "at the State-house door in his boots and spurs as the members were assembling; after a friendly salutation (without a word on the business) we went into the Hall of Congress together, and found we were among the latest: proceedings immediately commenced, and after a few minutes the great question was put; when the vote for Delaware was called, your uncle arose and said: 'As I believe the voice of my constituents and of all the sensible & honest men is in favor of Independence & my own judgment concurs with them I vote for Independence." Read voted nay but by a margin of two to one Delaware favored independence.

McKean did not get to sign the Declaration of Independence with his fellow members of Congress. Soon after casting his vote he led a militia group to assist George Washington during the unsuccessful defense of New York City. As a result of this military duty, McKean is considered to be the last signer of the Declaration of Independence. McKean insisted that he signed the document sometime in 1776 though most historians believe he affixed his signature to the document between 1777 and 1781.

The war years weren't quiet ones for McKean. He had been placed on the English hit list and wrote in a letter to John Adams that "he was being hunted like a fox." When the British captured the rebel governor of Delaware, McKean assumed the post. At the same time he was serving quite capably as Chief Justice of Pennsylvania in a post he filled from 1777 until 1799. According to his biographer John Coleman, "only the historiographical difficultly of reviewing court records and other scattered documents prevents recognition that McKean, rather than John Marshall, did more than anyone else to establish an independent judiciary in the United States. As Chief Justice under a Pennsylvania constitution he considered flawed, he assumed it the right of the court to strike down legislative acts it deemed unconstitutional, preceding by ten years the U.S. Supreme Court's establishment of the doctrine of judicial review."

In October of 1776 the during what was viewed as a conservative reaction against independence, the Delaware General Assembly did not re-elect McKean to the newly declared nation's Congress. Within a year British occupation of the state changed public opinion, and McKean was returned to Congress in 1777. He would serve in this body until 1783. He helped draft the Articles of Confederation and voted for their adoption in 1781. That same year he was elected to the position of President of Congress. Though primarily a ceremonial position with little authority some have argued that McKean served as President of the United States.

Though he did not attend the Constitutional Convention, McKean took a leading role in securing Pennsylvania's ratification of the United States Constitution. He argued in favor of a strong executive and was a member of the state convention that voted to ratify the document. When American political parties came into being, he allied himself initially with the Federalists. By the mid-1790s he broke with that party because of disagreements with compromises that the administration in Philadelphia made with Great Britain. He became an outspoken Jeffersonian Republican.

In 1799 McKean was elected to the first of three terms he would serve as Governor of Pennsylvania. As Governor, he demanded that

The grave of Thomas McKean

things be done his way. He removed his critics from government posts and rewarded his supporters with jobs. His administration was so stormy that he had to survive an impeachment attempt by his political foes in 1807. In this, he proved successful.

McKean passed away in 1817 at the age of 83. He was initially laid to rest in the First Presbyterian Church Cemetery, but his remains were moved to Philadelphia's Laurel Hill Cemetery in 1843. In a letter to one of McKean's sons, John Adams described his fellow founder as "among the best tried and firmest pillars of the Revolution."

McKean County, Pennsylvania is named in his honor. There is also a McKean Street in Philadelphia. Both the University of Delaware and Penn State University have buildings named for him.

Hugh Mercer
(1726–1777)

The Hero of Princeton

Buried at Laurel Hill Cemetery,
Philadelphia, Pennsylvania.

Military

Hugh Mercer, known as the Hero of Princeton, was a brigadier general in
the Continental Army who was a close friend of George Washington. A
doctor by trade, he was born in Scotland and served in the British military before emigrating to the colonies. During the American Revolution,
Mercer died from his wounds at the Battle of Princeton and was immor-
talized in famous paintings depicting the scene.

Hugh Mercer was born on January 16, 1726, at the manse of Pitsligo
Kirk, near Rosehearty in Aberdeenshire, Scotland. Mercer was the son
of the Pitsligo Parish Church of Scotland minister Reverend William
Mercer and his wife, Ann Monro. He began studying medicine at only
fifteen years of age, attending Marischal College at the University of
Aberdeen and later graduating as a doctor at only nineteen.

Mercer then served as an assistant surgeon in the army of Charles
Edward Stuart, also known as Bonnie Prince Charlie, who was a pre-
tender to the British throne and who led the Jacobite uprising to restore
the Stuarts to power. When the rebellion was crushed at Culloden on
April 16, 1746, the Hanoverian line under George II was preserved,
and Scotland was forced down the path of integration into the United

Hugh Mercer fighting for his life at Princeton

Kingdom. Many of the surviving Jacobites were hunted down and killed, and Mercer feared for his life. In 1747, after months of hiding from authorities, Mercer boarded a ship and moved to North America. He settled first in Franklin County, Pennsylvania, near the village of Black Town, now called Mercersburg in his honor. He practiced as a doctor there for the next eight years, far away from Philadelphia and any officials who might still be hunting Jacobites.

In 1755, at the outset of the French and Indian War, some claim Mercer was with Braddock when he was defeated at Fort Duquesne. Others claim he treated the many wounded from that debacle, but there is no record of Hugh fighting for the British until the following year, 1756.

That year, he was commissioned a captain in the Pennsylvania militia under Lt. Col. John Armstrong. The colonel led an expedition of 300 Pennsylvania provincial troops in September against the Indian village of Kittanning, forty miles northeast of modern-day Pittsburgh, Pennsylvania. During the raid, a victory for the provincials, Mercer was severely wounded and separated from his unit. He walked over 100 miles to Fort Shirley in (now) Huntingdon County, Pennsylvania, about fifty

The Death of General Mercer at the Battle of Princeton January 3, 1777 by John Trumbull

miles west of Carlisle, living off the land for a fortnight. Upon his return, Mercer was promoted to colonel and soon met another colonel, George Washington, with whom he became close friends.

⟫◈⟪

Mercer and Washington accompanied General John Forbes during the second attempt to capture Fort Duquesne in 1758. On November 25, the burned fort was occupied, and Forbes set about to construct a new fort to be named Fort Pitt after the British Secretary of State. The nearby settlement was dubbed Pittsburgh.

This whole time, General Forbes was in poor health and became gravely ill. In early December he returned to Philadelphia and left Mercer in command. Mercer first built a temporary fort, called Mercer's Fort, at the two forks in the Ohio River to prevent the return of the French. Today this site is a parking lot between Point State Park and the Pittsburgh Post-Gazette building.

Back in Philadelphia, General Forbes passed away on March 11, 1759, and was buried at Christ Church. Mercer continued his duties to secure the area for construction of Fort Pitt. Mercer was commended by the Commander-in-Chief of the British Army in North America, Sir Jeffrey Amherst, for his professionalism. Said Amherst, "Some such men as Colonel Mercer amongst the Provincials would be of great service . . ."

After the war, in 1760, Mercer relocated to Fredericksburg, Virginia, where there was a thriving Scottish community. There, he set up as a doctor and opened an apothecary which is now a museum at 1020 Caroline Street. Mercer became a prominent man in the community, purchasing tracts of land and becoming a member of the Fredericksburg Masonic Lodge of which he was soon Master. This same lodge also claimed George Washington and James Monroe as members as well as other generals during the American Revolution: George Weeden, William Woodford, Fielding Lewis, Thomas Posey, Gustavus Wallace, and (in 1824 as an honorary member) the Marquis de Lafayette. Mary Washington, George's mother, became a patient of Mercer's and he saw many other prominent members of the community.

Mercer married Isabella Gordon and had five children with her: Ann (who married Patton), John, William, George Weeden, and Hugh Tennant. In 1774, George Washington sold his childhood home, Ferry Farm, to Mercer who envisioned creating a town where he and his family would settle.

As tensions increased between the colonies and Great Britain, Mercer became a member of the Fredericksburg Committee of Safety in 1775. The day after Lexington and Concord in Massachusetts, the Royal Governor Dunmore of Virginia ordered the seizing of gunpowder in Williamsburg. This riled the local militias and Mercer was among those urging action. Though initially excluded for a military post by the Virginians due to being Scottish (Jacobite), on September 12, he was appointed a Colonel of the Virginia Minute Men covering Spotsylvania, King George, Stafford, and Caroline Counties, known as the Third Virginia Regiment. George Weedon was appointed lieutenant colonel. James Monroe and future Chief Justice of the United States John Marshall were officers under his command.

In June 1776 the Continental Congress appointed Mercer brigadier general and ordered him to report to New York. Mercer left his family and headed north to take on his new duties reporting to his friend, George Washington. That summer, while Washington was building Fort

Washington on the New York side of the Hudson River, Mercer over-saw the construction of Fort Lee on the New Jersey side. Unfortunately, this fort fell during the British attacks that November. As the beaten Continental Army retreated to New Jersey, the army was in crisis and in danger of being further decimated due to the large number of enlist-ments that were ending on January 1, 1777.

With only days until many of the troops would go home, it is said Mercer hatched the plan to cross the Delaware River and surprise the Hessians at Trenton. Certainly, Mercer was a significant contributor to its execution. Due to the victory on December 26, 1776, many of the soldiers agreed to stay on for ten more days provided they received a monetary bonus. This provided the window of opportunity for the Second Battle

Memorial to Hugh Mercer

of Trenton, also known as the Battle of Assunpink Creek, on January 2, 1777, when Washington defeated Cornwallis's 5000 troops. Mercer was tasked with helping defend the city from potential British capture.

With Cornwallis's forces split between Trenton and Princeton, Washington attacked the latter the following day, January 3. Mercer's brigade of 350 men was sent to destroy the Stony Brook Bridge but engaged with two British regiments and a mounted unit under Colonel Charles Manwood at Clarke's Orchard. Mistaken for George Washington, Mercer's horse was shot from under him, and he was surrounded and ordered to surrender. Mercer refused and drew his saber, and a struggle ensued that devolved to hand-to-hand combat as the men fought to secure the heights of a nearby hill. Unfortunately, most of Mercer's men did not have bayonets on their muskets like their counterparts. They began to fall back, but Mercer desperately rallied them with a cry of "Forward! Forward!" The Brits eventually got him to the ground and stabbed him seven times, leaving him for dead. According to legend, this occurred at a white oak tree which became known as the "Mercer Oak" which later became the seal of Mercer County, New Jersey.

With Mercer on the ground, the colonials retreated but ran into Washington who immediately rallied them upon learning of his friend's fate. They pushed back the British and recovered Mercer, who lay dying from the bayonet wounds and blows to his head. The mortally wounded Mercer was carried to the field hospital at the Thomas Clarke House, now a museum at 500 Mercer Road. Doctor Benjamin Rush attended to him, but Mercer succumbed nine days later, on January 12, 1777. He was initially buried at Christ Church in Philadelphia but was moved to Laurel Hill Cemetery in 1840.

Washington's army was victorious at Princeton, and Mercer's valiant effort became the rallying cry for the colonials whose enlistment problems abated. Following the victory, Washington camped in Morristown, and the Americans secured French arms and supplies. Cornwallis pulled his forces back to New York, stunned by the defeats. Back in London, British public support for the war began to wane.

Two famous paintings of the Revolution portray Mercer at Princeton. John Trumbull used Hugh Mercer, Jr., as the model for *The Death of General Mercer at the Battle of Princeton*. Charles Willson Peale painted

The original tombstone of Hugh Mercer

the mortally wounded Mercer in the background of his *Washington at the Battle of Princeton*. This painting is a prized possession of Princeton University.

Many Mercer descendants have distinguished themselves. His grandson, John Mercer Patton, was a governor of Virginia. His sons were Confederate officers Lt. Col. Walter T. Patton and Col. George Smith Patton. The latter was the grandfather of General George S. Patton, Jr., of World War II fame. Another grandson of Mercer, Hugh Weedon Mercer, was a Confederate general. The songwriter Johnny Mercer was a descendant as was Sergeant Christopher Mercer Lowe of the U.S. Army, who was recently killed while serving in Afghanistan.

Besides the Mercer Oak, Mercersburg, Pennsylvania, and Mercer County, New Jersey, Mercer's name has been affixed to five other counties across the country, to the town of Mercerville, New Jersey, and to a street in New York City. An elementary school in Fredericksburg, Virginia is also named after him. There is also a prominent statue of Mercer in that town.

Samuel Meredith
(1741–1817)

Silk Stockings Associator

Buried at Samuel Meredith Monument,
Pleasant Mount, Pennsylvania.

———•◦•———

Military • 1st Treasurer of U.S.A.

Samuel Meredith partnered with his father, Reese Meredith, and founder George Clymer in a successful merchant business in Philadelphia,
Meredith and Clymer. At the outset of the Revolution, Samuel enlisted
in the Continental Army and rose to brigadier general before returning
to his business pursuits. He then became a Continental Congressman
and later served as the first Treasurer of the post-Constitution United
States during the entire Washington and Adams administrations and the
beginning of the Jefferson administration, from 1789 to 1801.

———•◦•———

Born in Philadelphia, Pennsylvania, in 1741, Samuel Meredith
was the son of Reese Meredith (1705–1778) and his wife, Martha (née
Carpenter). The elder Meredith was from Leominster, Herefordshire,
England. He was educated at Oxford and married into the Carpenter
family of prosperous merchants. Reese and Martha emigrated to
Philadelphia in February 1730, following the death of his father, John
Meredith, where he later became a friend of George Washington.

Young Samuel attended Doctor Francis Allison's Academy in
Philadelphia before becoming engaged in mercantile pursuits. Allison

Samuel Meredith

also had as pupils Thomas McKean, George Read, James Smith, Charles Thomson, and the siblings of John Dickinson.

During the Stamp Act controversy of 1765, both Samuel and his father Reese signed the non-importation resolutions in Philadelphia that were similar to other protests throughout the colonies regarding "taxation without representation." During this time, Samuel partnered with his father and another Philadelphia merchant, George Clymer, to expand their enterprise, including the mercantile business and land speculation in northeastern Pennsylvania, Delaware, New York, Kentucky, and Virginia. Clymer later married Samuel's sister, Elizabeth, to further cement the relationship.

In 1772, Meredith married Margaret Cadwalader, the daughter of Doctor Thomas and Hannah Cadwalader. The father-in-law was a well-known physician who was also a member of the American Philosophical

Society. The Merediths had six children. A daughter, Martha, later married John Read, the son of Constitution and Declaration of Independence signer George Read.

By 1775, Meredith was involved in politics as a delegate to the Pennsylvania Provincial Congress, held in Philadelphia. He also served as the chairman of the Committee of Safety. After shots were fired that spring at Lexington and Concord, Meredith volunteered for military service. He was assigned to the 3rd Battalion of Associators, also known as the "Silk Stockings Company" because of the upper-class social standing of the men. As a major in this brigade, he saw action at the battles of Trenton and Princeton. He led a different brigade at the battles of Brandywine and Germantown, earning him a promotion to brigadier general. However, only a few months later, in January 1778, he resigned his commission and returned to Philadelphia to deal with the repercussions of the British invasion of that city on his family and property.

Meredith then served three terms in the Pennsylvania Colonial Assembly, from 1778 to 1779, 1781 to 1782, and 1782 to 1783. William Duer wrote to Robert Morris from Rhinebeck, New York on July 11, 1781:

> "I have just received your Favor of the 29th May on my Return last Night from Camp, where I had the Pleasure of seeing the Chevalier de la Luzerne, and our Mutual Friend Mr. Meredith."

That November, Meredith was elected as a director of the Bank of North America.

On October 31, 1786, Meredith, a Federalist, was appointed by the Pennsylvania legislature to the Continental Congress. He served through 1788, focusing mainly on financial matters. During this time, in December 1787, Meredith took in part in Pennsylvania's ratifying convention along with Thomas McKean, Anthony Wayne, Stephen Chambers, and Timothy Pickering.

With the new federal government underway in early 1789, Meredith petitioned President George Washington for a position:

"As the Unanimous voice of America will very soon call you to a Station which I flatter myself you will not decline filling, I hope this application (which perhaps I ought to have deferred till this universally wished for event had realy [*sic*] taken place) may not appear indelicate in your Eyes—The Fall of Landed property, added to losses occasioned by a too great confidence in Continental money, have so extreemly [*sic*] diminished my income as to render it necessary I should do something for the present support of my Family, I, therefore, take the Liberty of requesting the favour [sic] of your Interest in order to procure some office under Congress, in which I may be of service to the Publick [*sic*], & at the same time benefit myself—It is generally supposed the import will immediately in the meeting of Congress engage their attention, and as an Officer will be required for that department; I should esteem myself very fortunate if thro [*sic*] your Influence I could be appointed, and be assured Sir I shall endeavour by a faithful discharge of the duties of the Office to make some returns for the Obligation your friendship will lay me under on this particular occasion1—As for the unspeakable one I and all America owe you as the Preserver of your Country they must ever remain in full force."

President Washington appointed Meredith as the surveyor of the Port of Philadelphia on August 1, 1789, and then weeks later, nominated him to serve as the first Treasurer of the United States. With the Senate's consent, Meredith took office on September 11, 1789. During this time, Meredith was responsible for managing the money of the new republic, settling its many bills, working in concert with Secretary of the Treasury Alexander Hamilton. He often gave his personal funds to do so, including over a hundred thousand dollars never repaid to him or his heirs. He developed a system for managing his duties and was retained through the entire Washington and Adams administrations.

On October 31, 1801, only months after the inauguration of Thomas Jefferson as the third President of the United States, Meredith resigned his post. He had written Jefferson on August 29, 1801:

"The precarious state of Mrs. Meredith's health, which has been injured by change of situation, the anxious desire she and the family have to be with their Friends & relations, as well as the necessary attention to my private affairs, which are suffering by my absence from Philada.; have induced me to offer you my resignation, to take place if you think proper about the last of October, or beginning of November, which I think will give me time to receive returns from the most distant Banks, make up my Quarterly Accounts to the 30th: September, and hand them to the Auditor for settlement: And for you Sir, to fix on a successor, to whom I may deliver over the funds in my hands, giving him every information I am capable of . . ."

Upon leaving office on December 1, 1801, Meredith headed to his country estate, Belmont Manor, near Pleasant Mount, Wayne County, Pennsylvania. There he lived the rest of his days, passing on February 10, 1817, at the age of 65 or 66. Recorded one newspaper at the time:

"Meredith, at the commencement of the revolution, took an active and decided part with his country. A native of Philadelphia, he was among the foremost of the Patriots of that day who encountered hazards, and endured the privations, attendant on the crisis of the times, being personally engaged at the cannonade of Trenton, the battle of Princeton, and afterwards with his family suffering in exile on the occupation of Philadelphia by the British."

Meredith was initially laid to rest in the family plot at Belmont Manor. His wife, Margaret, followed in 1820.

In 1904, thanks to local efforts and a Commonwealth grant, Mr. and Mrs. Meredith's remains were removed to a plot in the town of Pleasant Mount, where a monument with a life-sized statue was erected to honor him. It reads, "Samuel Meredith. First Treasurer of the U.S.A."

The grave of Samuel Meredith

Said one of the speakers honoring Meredith at the dedication of the memorial:

"The name of Samuel Meredith 'was not born to die,' else we should not be here today, nearly a century after he breathed his last sign among the hills of Wayne, to unveil a monument to his memory. If that name had been doomed to oblivion, surely it would have long since passed from the minds of men. Rarely in the history of public benefactors has there been such tardy recognition of their merit as this demonstration discloses."

Thomas Mifflin
(1744–1800)

Governor Mifflin

Buried at Trinity Lutheran Church,
Lancaster, Pennsylvania.

———•◦•———

**Continental Association • U.S. Constitution • Military
President of Congress • First Governor of Pennsylvania**

Thomas Mifflin is a Founding Father of our country whose contributions have gone unheralded and are largely forgotten. He risked his life for American independence and democracy. He spent almost his entire life in public service. He was expelled from his church for fighting the British, served as President of the Continental Congress, was a signer of the U.S. Constitution, and was Pennsylvania's first governor. Despite his many accomplishments and his contributions as a Founding Father, there is no monument that identifies his grave. There is a roadside historical marker saying he is interred somewhere on the grounds of Trinity Lutheran Church. It is uncertain where precisely he is buried. In addition, there is little mention of his many distinguished accomplishments during his long life of service to his country and his state. One internet site claims the grave was paved over for a parking lot. There is a marble slab in the wall of the church that states he was a signer of the Constitution.

———◆◦◆———

Thomas Mifflin was born on January 10, 1744, in Philadelphia where his parents were prominent Quakers. He attended local schools

Thomas Mifflin

and in 1760, graduated from the College of Philadelphia (today known as the University of Pennsylvania). He went into business with a local merchant and in 1765, he formed a partnership in the import and export business with his younger brother.

Mifflin married a distant cousin, Sarah Morris, in 1771. That same year, he was elected city warden. In 1772, he began the first of four consecutive terms in the Colonial legislature. In the summer of 1774, Mifflin was elected by the legislature to the First Continental Congress. His work there spread his reputation across America and led to his election to the Second Continental Congress which convened in Philadelphia in the aftermath of the fighting at Lexington and Concord.

He played a major role in the creation of Philadelphia's militia and was commissioned as a major in May 1775. Despite his family being Quakers for generations, he was expelled from the church because military service violated the pacifist nature of the faith. In what had to be a difficult decision Mifflin viewed service to his country as more important than adherence to religious beliefs.

When Congress created the Continental Army in June 1775, Mifflin resigned from the militia to go on active duty with the regulars. George Washington, the Commander in Chief, selected Mifflin as one of his aides. Shortly after, Washington appointed him Quartermaster General of the Continental Army. His service as Quartermaster earned him a promotion to Brigadier General, but he longed for a field command and requested to be reassigned. He was transferred to the infantry and led a brigade of Pennsylvania continentals during the New York City campaign. He fought bravely in the battles of Long Island, Trenton, and Princeton, and was with Washington during the terrible winter at Valley Forge. Throughout this time his persuasive oratory convinced many men not to leave the military service. However, he was soon returned to the position of Quartermaster when no suitable replacement could be found for him. It was a move that left him bitterly disappointed.

In November 1776, General Mifflin was sent by Washington to Philadelphia to report to the Continental Congress on the critical condition of the army. The Continental Army was outgunned and outmanned and unable to make a stand in New Jersey to stop the advancing British march towards Philadelphia. It was a wise move by the Commander-in-Chief to send General Mifflin to rally Philadelphia, as Congress, in fear of losing the capital was preparing to take flight to Baltimore. When the Continental Army was forced into Pennsylvania, the citizens of Philadelphia began to panic. Business was suspended, schools were closed, and roads leading from the city were crowded with refugees all fleeing the city.

At a town meeting, General Mifflin addressed the crowd and much of the Continental Congress. After listening to Mifflin, Congress formally appealed to the militia of Philadelphia and surrounding areas to join Washington's army. Mifflin organized and trained three regiments of militia and sent 1,500 men to Washington. He also orchestrated a re-supply of Washington's desperate troops once they reached Valley Forge. These were critical components needed by Washington to cross the Delaware and attack the British in Trenton. In recognition of his services, Congress commissioned Mifflin as a major-general and made him a member of the Board of War.

On the Board of War, General Mifflin joined a growing number of delegates and generals who shared the dissatisfaction of General Washington's conduct of the war. He sympathized with the views of General Horatio Gates and General Thomas Conway who blamed Washington for the losses of the Continental Army. In the fall of 1777, Horatio Gates, with the help of Benedict Arnold, defeated the British forces at Saratoga. Almost immediately, Washington's enemies, emboldened by the victory, sought his replacement with the "Hero of Saratoga" General Gates. General Conway organized an effort to have the Board of War establish Gates as the new Commander-in-Chief. This became known as "The Conway Cabal." When the effort failed, Mifflin submitted his resignation. Congress refused to accept it, but he was discharged from the Board of War.

In late 1778, while still on active duty, he won re-election to the State Legislature. In 1780, he was again elected to the Continental Congress and in 1783, the Continental Congress elected him as President of the Congress. He presided over the ratification of the Treaty of Paris, which

Plaque honoring Thomas Mifflin where his grave is believed to be

ended the Revolution and ironically accepted Washington's formal resignation as Commander-in-Chief. In what many historians say was one of the most remarkable events of United States history, George Washington was formally received by President Thomas Mifflin and Congress. At the pinnacle of his power and popularity, Washington resigned his commission as Commander-in-Chief to the President of the Continental Congress, a man who had once conspired to replace him.

Mifflin represented Pennsylvania at the United States Constitutional Convention and was a signer of it. He presided over the committee that wrote Pennsylvania's first constitution which established a bicameral legislature with a strong governor. He then ran for governor in 1790 and was elected as Pennsylvania's first governor by a margin of almost ten to one. He served three terms as governor until 1799.

Thomas Mifflin died on January 20, 1800, in Lancaster and was buried in the cemetery of Trinity Lutheran Church at state expense since his estate was too small to cover funeral costs. The cemetery no longer exists. Most of the bodies were moved in the 1840s to Woodward Hill Cemetery, but Mifflin's was not. There is a historical marker on South Duke Street that says, "here are interred the remains of Thomas Wharton, Jr. and Governor Thomas Mifflin."

Gouverneur Morris
(1752–1816)

The Penman of the Constitution

Buried at Saint Ann's Episcopal Churchyard,
Bronx, New York.

Articles of Confederation • U.S. Constitution • Military • Diplomat

He was a founding father who hailed from New York City. He argued with his family over the issue of American independence. He served in the army during the Revolutionary War. He signed both the Articles of Confederation and the United States Constitution. He is credited with writing large sections of the latter document including the preamble. He was also a United States Senator from 1800 to 1803. His name was Gouverneur Morris.

Morris was born on January 31, 1752, in what is now called the Bronx section of New York City at the family estate known as Morrisania Manor. As a boy, he exhibited a keen intellect. So keen in fact that, at the age of twelve, he enrolled in King's College which is now known as Columbia University. He began his studies in 1764 and graduated in four years. Since he was too young at age sixteen to start a career, he stayed at King's and received his Master's degree in 1771. Next Morris studied under the noted New York law scholar William Smith. It was through Smith, who opposed British tax policies in the colonies, that Morris met patriots such as John Jay and Alexander Hamilton.

Gouverneur Morris

In 1775, Morris was elected to the New York Provincial Congress. This Congress was organized by patriots who were seeking an alternative to the Province of New York Assembly, which was the official pro-British body. It was during his service in the Provincial Congress that Morris began supporting turning the colony of New York into an independent state. This put him at odds with both his family and his mentor William Smith who had turned away from the patriot cause when it moved towards pursuing independence.

When the Revolutionary War began, Morris favored reasoning with those Americans who stayed loyal to the king. This is hardly surprising since this group, known as Tories, included his mother and his half-brother. His mother gave the family estate to the British army to be used for military purposes. As the war went on, Morris changed his views on the treatment of Tories and favored tarring and feathering, whippings and the confiscation of property.

In 1778, Morris was appointed to be a delegate to the Continental Congress. He was placed on a committee charged with reforming the Continental Army. Upon visiting the army at Valley Forge, he was so affected by the conditions that he became a spokesman for the military in Congress and was instrumental in reforms in training, methods, and financing. That same year, the Conway Cabal took place. Its purpose was to remove George Washington as Commander-in-Chief of the army. Morris cast the deciding vote that kept Washington in his job. In 1779, Morris was defeated in an election that cost him his seat in Congress. Most likely the defeat was caused by his support for a strong central government, a view not popular in New York at the time. After his defeat, he left New York and moved to Philadelphia.

In 1780, Morris shattered his left leg, and it had to be amputated. He said he had done it by getting his leg stuck in the spokes of a carriage he was driving. However, Morris had a reputation for having affairs with both married and unmarried women. There was gossip that the accident occurred while a jealous husband was chasing him.

In Philadelphia, he served as superintendent of finance from 1781 to 1785. He also worked as a merchant who put him in contact with the financier and founding father, Robert Morris (no relation). With the support of both George Washington and Robert Morris, he was appointed to be a Pennsylvania delegate to the 1787 Constitutional Convention.

Morris certainly made his presence known at the Convention. According to Catherine Drinker Bowen in her book *Miracle at Philadelphia*, Morris has been described as the most brilliant man at the Convention. She noted that he often spoke, giving 173 speeches, while never saying anything foolish or tedious. She describes his tactics as abrupt, first an eloquent explosive expression of his position and then cynically waiting for the Convention to catch up with him. He continued to favor a strong central government. He said, "When the powers of the national government clash with the states, only then must the states yield." Many others at the Convention, including Washington, shared his desire for a strong central government. Morris served on the Committee of Style and Arrangement who drafted the final language of the proposed constitution. Bowen called Morris the Committee's "amanuensis" meaning that he was responsible for most of the draft, as well as its final form. Also, Morris was one of the few delegates at the convention who spoke openly against slavery. According to James Madison's notes, Morris attacked slavery calling it a nefarious institution. After the Constitution was adopted, Morris was proud to put his signature on it. He then moved back to New York.

Morris went to France on business in 1789. He would not return for a decade. He served as Minister Plenipotentiary to France from 1792 to 1794. His diaries from this period have become a valuable resource concerning the French Revolution. They also help to document his ongoing affairs with women. He was openly critical of the French Revolution which led to a request from the French government to recall him which the United States eventually did.

Upon his return to the States, he resumed his law practice and entered politics. In 1800 he was elected to the United States Senate as a Federalist representing New York. He would serve until 1803. During this time, he championed improving transportation from the eastern part of the country to the interior. After being defeated in his reelection bid, he became Chairman of the Erie Canal Commission from 1810 to 1813. The canal was instrumental in transforming New York into a financial capital. That much was clear to Morris when he said: "The proudest empire in Europe is but a bubble compared to what America will be, must be, in the course of two centuries, perhaps of one."

Morris married at the age of 57. His wife was Ann Cary Randolph, the sister of Thomas Mann Randolph who was the husband of Thomas Jefferson's daughter Martha. Morris and his wife had one son, Gouverneur Morris Jr., who became a railroad executive.

On November 16, 1816, Morris passed away after causing himself internal injuries while using a piece of whalebone to clear a blockage in his urinary tract. He was laid to rest in Saint Ann's Episcopal Churchyard Cemetery along with his brother Lewis Morris who signed the Declaration of Independence.

Morris's grandson, William Walton Morris, a graduate of West Point, was a brevet Major General during the Civil War. He is also buried at Saint Ann's.

Monument to Morris in the Bronx. His grave is beneath the
church nearby.

During the early twentieth century, a great-grandson, also named
Gouverneur Morris (1876–1953), authored novels and short stories. The
Lon Chaney film *The Penalty* (1920) was adapted from one of them.

Morris was a substantial landowner in St. Lawrence County in up-
state New York. There, the town and village of Gouverneur are named
for him. During World War II, the liberty ship S.S. *Gouverneur Morris*
was named after him.

In *Pennsylvania History* in July 1938, Philip Wild summed up Morris's life:

> Endowed with all that aids a man to achieve much for the common good, namely sterling character, wisdom, worthwhile place and wealth, Morris, on the contrary, chose to use these gifts to advance and strengthen the position of the small group of property men to which he belonged, instead of setting for his goal, the securing of the greatest good for all the people. His narrow conservatism led to his failure to secure political gifts from the people about whom he so often manifested his lack of faith. Lacking political backing, Morris became embittered and adopted positions which have brought rather caustic criticisms to him from historians. But it must be remembered that in public office, his efforts controlled as they were by the more liberal tendencies of his higher officers, produced much of significance for the United States.

Robert Morris
(1734–1806)

Revolutionary Financier

Buried at Christ Episcopal Churchyard,
Philadelphia, Pennsylvania.

**Declaration of Independence • Articles of Confederation
U.S. Constitution • Finance**

This founder was once considered the wealthiest man in the country. He gave of his wealth willingly for the Revolution he helped bring about during his service in the Continental Congress. His signature can be found on the Declaration of Independence, the Articles of Confederation, and the United States Constitution. Along with George Washington and Benjamin Franklin, he is still widely viewed as one of the three men who made American Independence possible. He is also regarded as one of the founders of the financial system of the United States. For three years he served as the Superintendent of Finance, a time during which he was the central civilian in the government and considered by many to be, next to George Washington, the most powerful man in the country. He represented Pennsylvania in the United States Senate. Despite his widely successful career in business he spent over three years in debtor's prison and passed away in poverty. His name was Robert Morris.

Morris was born in Liverpool, England on January 20, 1734. His father was an ironmonger in Liverpool prior to emigrating to America to

Robert Morris

establish a tobacco shipping company in Oxford, Maryland. This business proved successful and when Morris reached the age of 13 he joined his father in America. In 1750 the elder Morris took a small boat in order to board a ship called the *Liverpool Merchant* to follow the custom of welcoming the captain to America. That task completed, he climbed back into the little boat to return to shore. The captain, also following the custom at the time, readied the ship's cannon to fire a salute. An insect, possibly a fly, landed on the captain's nose and he raised his arm to chase it away. The crew viewed this action as a signal to fire the cannon which they did prematurely. Morris, Sr., who was only 20 yards away, was struck by wadding which broke his right arm. The wound developed an infection and he died six days later leaving his considerable fortune to his son.

The suddenly wealthy Morris had been educated in Philadelphia where he became an apprentice to a merchant and mayor of the city, Charles Willing. The mayor died in 1854 and his son made Morris a partner in the firm. In 1757 the two young businessmen formed a shipping and banking firm. They would remain partners until 1779.

In 1769 at the age of 35, Morris married the 20-year-old Mary White. The couple would produce seven children; five sons, and two daughters. White came from a well-respected Maryland family. Her brother, William White, was a well-known Episcopal Bishop. Morris worshipped at St. Peter's Church in Philadelphia which was run by his brother in law. When the Continental Congress was in session many of its members also worshipped there.

As a leading merchant in one of America's most important cities, Morris could not escape the political issues of the day. Though he did not believe the time was right for independence, he took the side of the colonies in the struggle with England. In 1774 he signed on to boycott the importation of British goods despite the damage it would do to his business.

In 1775 Morris was appointed to the Continental Congress. Here he put his business experience to work for the American cause. As a member of the committee for commerce, he worked to supply the Continental Army with supplies by paying for them with shipments of American goods. Still, as of July 1, 1776, he wasn't ready to vote for American independence. On that day he cast a preliminary vote opposing separating from England.

On July 2, 1776, when the official vote was taken he abstained so that Pennsylvania would not be the only colony that failed to support the measure. Once the measure was passed, he became an ardent supporter of American independence and on August 2, 1776, he signed the Declaration of Independence. Regarding this act, he said, "I am not one of those politicians that run testy when my own plans are not adopted. I think it is the duty of a good citizen to follow when he cannot lead."

There are numerous examples of the work Morris did that earned him the title "Financer of the Revolution." One of the most important of these occurred after Washington crossed the Delaware on his way to victory in the Battle of Trenton. As General Howe's British and German Hessian troops retreated, the American general was being urged to pursue and strike the enemy in order to capitalize on his recent victory. Washington's problem was that his battle-hardened New England recruits' enlistments were ending and they were due to go home. Washington sent a messenger to Morris asking him to gather enough money to pay each soldier a ten-dollar bonus for extending their enlistment for six weeks. Since Washington wanted the funds to return with the messenger, Morris immediately went to work using his own funds and his own credit to fulfill Washington's request. In addition, Morris had heard that the general was also low on wine so in addition to the requested funds he sent along a quarter cask of good vintage. Using the funds Morris provided, Washington was able to keep the New Englanders in the army. It seemed that every time Washington was short on cash, Morris was able to find it. It has been reported that Morris gave one million of his own money to fund the decisive Yorktown campaign.

By the time the Revolution ended, Morris had already signed the Articles of Confederation creating a loose and ineffective union of the thirteen former colonies. In 1781, Congress named him the Superintendent of Finance. Only days after taking this position, Morris proposed the establishment of a national bank. The Bank of North America was the first financial institution chartered by the United States. The funding for the bank came, in part, through a loan from France which Morris had worked to obtain. He served as the Superintendent until 1784.

In 1787 Morris was one of Pennsylvania's representatives at the Constitutional Convention meeting in Philadelphia. On May 13th of that year Morris, now considered the richest man in the country, welcomed his old friend General Washington to Philadelphia and walked with him to his temporary residence where the General settled in comfortably in one of the city's grand mansions. On May 25th it was Morris who nominated Washington to be the President of the Convention. Though he attended the Constitutional Convention regularly, his participation was rare in that he spoke only twice and one of those occasions was nominating Washington. When the convention concluded, he added his name to the Constitution and worked for its ratification.

Some historians say that Washington wanted Morris to be the first Secretary of the Treasury but that the Pennsylvanian declined and recommended Alexander Hamilton who supported many of the policies that Morris had championed as the Superintendent of Finance. Morris was elected to the Senate and served in the first Congress. As a senator, he supported the Federalist agenda and strongly backed Hamilton's financial proposals. When some of his fellow members of that initial Congress expressed their frustration at what they viewed as slowness and inefficiency of the new government in accomplishing tasks, Morris disagreed. Older than many of his peers, Morris stated, "I have so often seen good consequences arise from public debate and discussion that I am not amongst the number of those who complain of the delay."

Morris, like several other founders, was heavily involved in land speculation schemes. Unfortunately, in his case, a number were unsuccessful, and he found himself unable to sell his western properties or pay the taxes on them. Many of those who witnessed the spectacular rise of Morris to the wealthiest man on the continent now watched a fall that was no less spectacular. Hounded by his creditors he was arrested and placed in a Philadelphia debtors' prison from February 1798 to August of 1801. In 1946 the *Harrisburg Evening News* reported that a review

The grave of Robert Morris

of his papers showed that Morris paid $1.25 a week for his board in his cell during his stay there. In 1800 Congress passed the temporary Bankruptcy Act which once enacted resulted in his release. The act was passed, at least in part to get Morris out of prison.

After his release, Morris was in ill health and was cared for by his wife for the rest of his days. He passed away May 8, 1806, and was laid to rest in the family vault of his brother in law Bishop William White in what is now the Christ Episcopal Church and Churchyard in Philadelphia. If you visit you will see a plaque placed by the Pennsylvania Constitution Commemorative Committee that notes his service during the Constitutional Convention. There is clearly far more to the story of this founder who went from being the richest man in America to a founder who, according to an April 19, 1939 article in the *Pittsburgh Post-Gazette*, submitted "with patience and fortitude" to poverty.

John Morton
(1724–1777)

Pennsylvania's Swing Vote

Buried at St. Paul's Burying Ground,
Chester, Pennsylvania.

———•—•———

Continental Association • Declaration of Independence

John Morton was an important Founding Father of the United States. He was elected to both the First and Second Continental Congress and was a signatory to the Continental Association and the U.S. Declaration of Independence. He provided the swing vote that allowed Pennsylvania to vote in favor of independence.

———◆—◆———

He was born in 1724 in Ridley Township, Pennsylvania. His father died just before he was born and not much is known about his childhood, not even the month or day of his birth. Both sides of his family emigrated from Sweden or Finland. His mother remarried an Englishman, John Sketchley, who played an important role in his development. He attended formal school for only about 3 months but thanks to his stepfather he would grow up to be a farmer, a surveyor, a lawyer, and a judge.

In 1748, Morton married Ann Justis. The couple had nine children and was active in the Anglican Church in Chester County. His public service began in 1756 when he was elected to the Pennsylvania Assembly. The next year he was also appointed justice of the peace, an office he held until 1764. He was one of four Pennsylvania delegates to the Stamp Act Congress in 1765. This congress is generally viewed as one of the first organized and coordinated political actions of the American Revolution. It was the first gathering of elected representatives from the colonies to devise a unified protest against new British taxation.

John Morton

In 1766, after ten years of service in the Pennsylvania Assembly, Morton gave up his seat to become the sheriff of Chester County. He was appointed sheriff after the incumbent sheriff, his close friend, died. He was reelected sheriff in 1767 and again in 1768. In 1769 he gave up the sheriff position and returned to the Pennsylvania Assembly. In 1774 he was elected Speaker of the Pennsylvania Assembly and elected to be a delegate to the First Continental Congress in Philadelphia. It was in October of that year when Congress formed the Continental Association. The Association signified the increasing cooperation between the colonies. As a sign of the desire still prevalent at the time, to avoid open revolution, the Association notably opened with a profession of allegiance to the king, and they placed the blame for " a ruinous system of colony administration" upon Parliament. The result called for implementing a trade boycott of Great Britain. Congress hoped that by imposing economic sanctions, they would pressure Great Britain into redressing the grievances of the colonies, in particular repealing the Intolerable Acts passed by the British Parliament. The Association aimed to alter Britain's policies towards the colonies without severing allegiance. Morton was one of seven Pennsylvania delegates to sign.

The next year he was again elected to the Second Continental Congress where he played a key role. As the Congress moved toward declaring independence, the Pennsylvania delegation was divided. Pennsylvania was considered a crucial state in this effort. Morton was undecided as the vote was approaching. Benjamin Franklin and James Wilson were aye votes. Thomas Willing and Charles Humphreys were nays. When Morton decided to vote aye on July 2, two other delegates,

John Dickinson and Robert Morris chose to absent themselves and thus Pennsylvania cast its vote for independence. He signed the historic document on August 2 with most of the other delegates. As a result of this vote, many friends, relatives, and neighbors turned against him.

Later that year Morton became Chairman of the Committee of The Whole and was heavily involved in writing the Articles of Confederation, the new nation's first form of government. In early 1777 he became very ill with what is suspected to have been tuberculosis and died on April 1. He was the first signer of the Declaration of Independence to die.

He was buried in Old St. Paul's Burial Ground also known as the Old Swedish Burial Ground, in the city of Chester, Pennsylvania. His grave remained unmarked until October 1845, when the present obelisk was erected by his descendants. When we first visited his grave the place showed shameful signs of neglect. The grounds were badly overgrown, many of the graves deteriorated, and the flag over Morton's grave in tatters. A second visit revealed some improvement.

The grave of John Morton

Frederick Augustus Conrad Muhlenberg
(1750–1801)

The First Speaker

Buried at Woodward Hill Cemetery,
Lancaster, Pennsylvania.

1st Speaker of the House

Frederick Augustus Conrad Muhlenberg was a Lutheran minister who was the son of Henry Melchior Muhlenberg, the founder of the Lutheran church in America. Frederick was also the grandson of Conrad Weiser, the colonial Indian agent, and interpreter. He was also the brother of Major General Peter Muhlenberg. During the American Revolution, Frederick Muhlenberg served in the Continental Congress representing Pennsylvania. He later served in Pennsylvania's Constitutional Convention and was subsequently elected to the First Congress of the U.S. House of Representatives. There he was elected the first Speaker of the House of the United States.

Frederick Muhlenberg was born January 2, 1750, in Trappe, Philadelphia (now Montgomery) County, Pennsylvania to the Reverend Henry Melchior Muhlenberg and his wife Anna Maria (née Weiser) Muhlenberg. Henry's father, Claus Nicholas Melchior Muhlenberg, hailed from Einbeck, in Hanover (Germany) where Prince George Louis was born. Prince George ascended the English throne as King George I.

Frederick Muhlenberg

Henry was a shoemaker, lay deacon, and town councilor. Henry studied theology and was ordained as a minister in the Lutheran Church. He answered a call from three congregations in Pennsylvania—at Philadelphia, Trappe, and New Hanover. He arrived in Philadelphia on November 25, 1742, and soon settled at Trappe. On April 22, 1745, Henry married Anna Maria Weiser, the daughter of Pennsylvania's colonial Indian agent and interpreter Conrad Weiser (1696-1760), who lived in Womelsdorf, Pennsylvania. The couple had three sons and four daughters.

Reverend Henry was busy with his calling and devoted little time to his sons. When Henry left his family behind in Trappe in 1761 to relocate to Philadelphia, the three sons were sent to be educated at the University of Halle in Germany under the tutelage of Dr. Francke. Frederick studied theology and foreign languages. In September 1770, Frederick returned to Philadelphia with his brother Gotthilf where he was ordained a minister in the Lutheran Church. Soon after, on October 15, 1771, Frederick married Catharine Schafer, the daughter of a Philadelphia sugar refiner.

Frederick's first assignment was assisting his brother-in-law, the Reverend Christian Emanuel Schulze, at the congregation in Tulpehocken (Womelsdorf), Pennsylvania. He also helped at congregations at Schaefferstown, Brickerville, White Oak, and Manheim until 1774. He then worked in Stouchsburg and Lebanon, Pennsylvania. Regarding the life of a traveling preacher, a descendant, Henry Melchior Muhlenberg Richards, wrote in 1902:

> We, of this age and comfort and conveniences, can hardly realize what the godly men of that day were called upon to endure in the performance of their ordinary duties. Some faint idea of their sacrifices may be gained by a perusal of the account left by Frederick of his trip from the Tulpehocken Valley to Shamokin, in the summer of 1771, to visit a little flock of German Lutherans there located, who were without pastor or church. He tells of his lonely ride through the wilds of the Blue Mountains, and beyond, with his one companion, young Conrad Weiser, the son of his Uncle Frederick; how he passed Fort Henry, already in a dilapidated condition . . . of the beautiful view which stretched before him from the top of the ridge: of the steep and dangerous paths, in one instance a mere shelf of the mountain . . .

The next two years, as the American Revolution unfolded, Frederick transferred to Christ Church in New York City. There he assisted Reverend Bernhard Michael Hausihl, who preached only in English. Frederick delivered prayers in German, which pleased the immigrant community.

By 1776, many in the congregation and Hausihl sided with the British while Muhlenberg sympathized with the Americans. They asked that Muhlenberg leave the church and return when the difficulties were concluded. In May 1776, with the British about to take New York City, the Muhlenbergs fled southward. His family went ahead to Philadelphia where Catharine had their third child. Frederick joined them on July 2, two days before the Declaration of Independence.

While brother Peter had become a colonel in the Continental Army, Frederick moved his family to Trappe where he delivered a sermon to a gathering of Continental troops saying, "Be not ye afraid of them; remember the Lord, which is great and terrible, and fight for your brethren, your sons, and your daughters, your wives, and your houses."

As the British next invaded Philadelphia, Frederick witnessed the defeats at Brandywine and Germantown. In early 1777, he took over the congregation at New Hanover (Falkner's Swamp) and continued for two more years in addition to serving at New Goshenhoppen and Oley.

During this time, Muhlenberg came to support the American Revolution more openly. On March 2, 1779, he was elected to the Continental Congress along with John McClene and Henry Wynkoop, joining Edward Biddle, Daniel Roberdeau, and William Clingan to represent Pennsylvania.

In 1780, Muhlenberg left the Continental Congress when he was elected to a seat in the Pennsylvania Assembly. He served as the Speaker of the Assembly from 1780 to 1783.

In 1787, Muhlenberg was a delegate at the Pennsylvania state constitutional convention which ratified the U.S. Constitution. He was then elected to the U.S. House of Representatives. On his first day in office, he was overwhelmingly elected by the members as the first Speaker of the House. This was arranged as a prize for Pennsylvania due to Virginia having the presidency (George Washington) and Massachusetts having the vice presidency (John Adams).

Muhlenberg served as the Speaker for the first Congress from 1789 to 1791. During this period, the Bill of Rights was passed and sent to the states for ratification. As Speaker, Muhlenberg was the first to sign it. During these formative times, there was a debate about how to address the president. John Adams, as vice president and president of the Senate, suggested such sobriquets as "His High Mightiness" and "His Elected Majesty." According to legend, it was Muhlenberg who suggested, "Mr. President."

For the Second Congress, Jonathan Trumbull of Connecticut was elected to the position but only held it for one term. During this time, on December 15, 1792, Muhlenberg, along with Senator James Monroe and Congressman Abraham Venable, confronted Secretary of the Treasury Alexander Hamilton about the Reynold's Affair, a sex and bribery scandal in which he was embroiled. Hamilton admitted the sordid details of the affair with Mrs. Reynolds but denied any financial impropriety and the three men agreed to keep the matter private. However, James Monroe later shared the letters with Hamilton's rival, Thomas Jefferson, who, five years later, exposed them to embarrass Hamilton. This nearly led to a duel between Hamilton and Monroe, ironically stopped by Aaron Burr's intervention.

Muhlenberg was reelected as Speaker for the third Congress from 1793 to 1795. In 1794, Muhlenberg abstained as the House voted 42-41 against a proposal to translate some of the national laws into German. Said Muhlenberg later, "the faster the Germans become Americans, the better it will be." He was subsequently tagged with the Muhlenberg Legend which claimed he was responsible for preventing German from becoming the official language of the United States.

The grave of Frederick Muhlenberg

Detail of Frederick's grave

During the fourth Congress, Muhlenberg yielded the speakership to Jonathan Dayton of New Jersey while retaining chairmanship of the Committee of the Whole. There, he cast the deciding vote on April 29, 1796, in support of the Jay Treaty with England, which was unpopular with the Jeffersonians. Muhlenberg was not reelected to the house and left on March 3, 1797.

His national political career over, Muhlenberg returned to Trappe where he served as president of the Council of Censors in Pennsylvania, a government oversight body with the power to suggest amendments to the state constitution and to censure government officials. In 1800, Muhlenberg was appointed as the receiver-general of the Pennsylvania Land Office.

Frederick Muhlenberg died suddenly on June 4, 1801, while attending to his duties in Lancaster, then the state capital. Said the *Lancaster Intelligencer* soon after, "At 11 o'clock on the Tuesday preceding his death, he repaired from his own house to the office of the surveyor-Gen., to attend a meeting of the board of property. He was then in his usual state of high health; but in less than an hour from that time, he was suddenly seized with a violent apoplectic fit; to which his plethorick [sic] habit and extreme corpulence had, perhaps, predisposed him. This stroke was soon succeeded by two others, of greater severity; and within 50 hours from the

The Speaker's house in Trappe, Pennsylvania, during the restoration

first attack, his dissolution took place." The article followed with a glowing obituary of his contributions to the commonwealth and the nation.

Frederick Muhlenberg was first buried at Trinity Lutheran Church in Lancaster, where Thomas Mifflin and Thomas Wharton had been recently buried. Muhlenberg was later reinterred at Woodward Hill Cemetery in Lancaster after its founding in 1850. His gravestone makes no mention of his national service. Muhlenberg's house in Trappe, known as the Speaker's House, is a museum administered by the local historical society.

Wrote John Adams about the Muhlenberg brothers, Frederick and Peter, "These two Germans, who had been long in public affairs and in high offices, were the great leaders and oracles of the whole German interest in Pennsylvania and the neighboring States . . . The Muhlenbergs turned the whole body of the Germans, great numbers of the Irish, and many of the English, and in this manner introduced the total change that followed in both Houses of the Legislature, and in all the executive departments of the national government. Upon such slender threads did our elections then depend!"

Muhlenberg Township in Berks County, Pennsylvania, is named after Frederick Muhlenberg as was the World War II liberty ship S.S. *F.A.C. Muhlenberg.*

John Peter Gabriel Muhlenberg
(1746–1807)

The Minister Who Became a General

Buried at Augustus Lutheran Church Cemetery,
Trappe, Pennsylvania.

Major General

John Peter Gabriel Muhlenberg was a Lutheran minister who was the son of Henry Melchior Muhlenberg, the founder of the Lutheran church in America. He was also the grandson of Conrad Weiser, the colonial Indian agent, and interpreter. In addition, he was the brother of the first Speaker of the House of Representatives, Frederick Muhlenberg. During the American Revolution, Peter Muhlenberg served in the Continental Army, rising to the level of Major General at the war's end. He later served in the U.S. House of Representatives for four terms and briefly in the U.S. Senate.

Peter Muhlenberg was born October 1, 1746, in Trappe, Philadelphia (now Montgomery) County, Pennsylvania to the Reverend Henry Melchior Muhlenberg and his wife, Anna Maria (née Weiser) Muhlenberg. (Further details of Peter's siblings, parents, and grandparents can be found in the preceding chapter about his brother, Frederick Muhlenberg.)

While Peter's younger brothers, Frederick and Gotthilf, continued their studies in Germany, by 1767 the elder Peter tired of academics and ran off to join the British 60th Regiment of Foot. He also served briefly

Peter Muhlenberg

in a military unit of German dragoons earning the nickname "Teufel Piet" (Devil Pete) and worked as a sales assistant for a grocer in Lübeck. Peter rose to the secretary of the German regiment, but his parents disapproved and recalled him to Philadelphia.

Back home in 1767, he received a classical education at the Academy of Philadelphia, now the University of Pennsylvania. He became an ordained minister in the Lutheran church in 1768 and moved to Bedminster, New Jersey to lead the congregation there as well as the one in New Germantown. Soon after, he transferred to Woodstock, Virginia. There, in 1770, he married the daughter of a successful potter, Anna Barbara "Hannah" Meyer. The two ultimately had six children.

Due to the Anglican Church being the state church of Virginia, Peter was also required to be ordained in that church. On a visit to England in 1772, he achieved that goal, though he served a Lutheran congregation of German immigrants.

By 1774, as the rumblings of the Revolution were in the air, Muhlenberg was elected to the House of Burgesses, was a delegate to the

First Virginia Convention, and led his local Committee of Safety and Correspondence in Dunmore County.

Late in 1775, though discouraged by his brother Frederick, upon the personal urging of George Washington, Muhlenberg raised the 8th Virginia Regiment of the Continental Army and served as its colonel. Many of the soldiers in the regiment were German immigrants. At only 29, Muhlenberg was the youngest of the eight Virginia colonels and had more military experience than only Patrick Henry.

According to a biographer in the mid-1800s who was related to Muhlenberg, on January 21, 1776, he gave a sermon to his congregation in Woodstock, Virginia, quoting from Ecclesiastes, "To everything, there is a season . . . a time of war, and a time of peace." He then declared, "And this is the time of war," while removing his clerical robe to reveal his officer's uniform beneath. Immediately, over 162 men were moved to enroll in the regiment, kissed their wives, and enlisted. By the next day, 300 had joined. While historians accept that Muhlenberg formed and led the regiment, they doubt the account of the sermon given its provenance and the lack of reports of such an event before the biography.

The 8th Virginia Regiment was initially sent to Charleston, South Carolina. They first saw combat on June 28, 1776, at the defense of Sullivan Island, off the coast of Charleston. Charles Lee, the American commander, reported concerning the Virginia troops, they were "brave to the last degree," and later added "I know not which corps I have the greatest reason to be pleased with Muhlenberg's Virginians, or the North Carolina troops—they are both equally alert, zealous, and spirited."

On February 1, 1777, the Continental Congress promoted Muhlenberg to brigadier general and ordered him to join the army of George Washington near Philadelphia serving under Nathanael Greene's division at Valley Forge. He was given command of all the Virginia regiments, known as the Virginia Line on May 26, 1777.

Muhlenberg's units were known to be well-disciplined. Washington chose Muhlenberg that August to lead the troops through Philadelphia to confront Howe's invasion force because he felt Muhlenberg's units would make the best impression on the local citizenry.

On September 11, 1777, serving under Nathanael Greene at the Battle of Brandywine, Muhlenberg's troops were not in a position to engage and did not see any action in the American defeat. However, the next month, on October 3 at Germantown, Muhlenberg's forces were among those on the frontlines. One general remembered them "advancing with spirit . . ." Another Continental officer recorded, "Muhlenberg and Scott, pressing forward with eagerness, encountered and broke a part of the British right-wing, entered the village, and made a considerable number of prisoners." Unfortunately, this did not last long. A fog fell upon the field, causing confusion among the units, especially near the Chew House. Muhlenberg's troops held their ground firing their muskets but began to run out of ammunition requiring them to withdraw. William Johnson, Nathanael Greene's biographer, later wrote of the bravery shown by Muhlenberg's Virginia Line saying it was "the only part of the American army that had the good fortune to effect the service allotted it that day."

During the retreat from Germantown, Muhlenberg's brigade was the rearguard and was among the last to leave the field. According to a later biography, Muhlenberg was with the rearguard and was weary from battle. He fell asleep on his horse only to be awakened by the whistle of a British musket ball. He awoke to see a British officer directing his men toward him, drew his pistol and fired, hitting the enemy leader.

The next spring, on March 2, 1778, Muhlenberg was irritated by a decision of a board of his fellow generals when they recognized William Woodford, who had left for a time and returned, as his senior among the Virginia Line officers. Muhlenberg threatened to resign and received support from Washington in the matter. Congress smoothed things over by stating, "the change in seniority was not intended to reflect upon the personal characters or comparative merits of those officers."

During the remainder of 1778 and 1779, Muhlenberg's brigades saw no action though they were present for the attack at Stony Point and were likely at the Battle of Monmouth. During the winter of 1780, most of the Virginia Line was sent south to defend Charleston, but Muhlenberg was given command of all forces in Virginia. However, the state treasury was bare, and there were few troops. Muhlenberg was tasked with raising and training militia units to resist the pending British incursions into the state.

In October 1780, near Portsmouth, Muhlenberg led a small brigade of only 800 raw militia to challenge a much larger British force who fell back and dug in. Muhlenberg was then reinforced by 5000 militia who surrounded the British. By the end of the month, the invaders decided to return to their ships.

Washington next sent Major General Baron von Steuben to Virginia in December 1780 given the increase in enemy activity. Muhlenberg now reported to him, and the two developed a rapport.

Not long after von Steuben arrived, British Brigadier General Benedict Arnold landed at Portsmouth with 2,000 soldiers and began marching inland. Muhlenberg again rallied his militia and once again cornered the enemy at Portsmouth. Rather than attack directly with his inferior force, Muhlenberg continued to harass the enemy until more aid came.

In response, Washington sent Marquis de Lafayette and 1,200 men as reinforcements to attack from land while the French navy attempted to cut off escape by sea. This plot was foiled when the French fleet was defeated by the British. The British then reinforced their position with more troops from New York.

As the pressure mounted from the increasing number of invaders, von Steuben ordered Muhlenberg further inland. On April 24, 1781, the 1,000 American troops encountered 2,500 British soldiers outside of Petersburg. Von Steuben ordered Muhlenberg to establish a defensive position to delay the enemy. These militia units were not as disciplined as the regular units of the Virginia Line, but the men fought well as they retreated. Von Steuben later reported, "General Muhlenberg merits my particular acknowledgments for the good disposition which he made and the great gallantry with which he executed it."

As 1781 proceeded, more attention was focused on the coastal area of Virginia. Washington and his French ally Rochambeau marched to Virginia to attack British General Cornwallis. Muhlenberg was assigned to a brigade of Continentals in Lafayette's Light Division. On September 29, 1781, the allies began their siege of Yorktown.

Over two weeks later, on October 14, Major Alexander Hamilton led a battalion of Muhlenberg's and two from Moses Hazen's brigade to the

The grave of Peter Muhlenberg

climactic attack on the British defenses. The rest of Muhlenberg's and
Hazen's forces then followed the successful attack, arriving as Hamilton
went over the works. The American and French victory at Yorktown
marked the end of the major fighting in the Revolutionary War. It was
the last military action for Muhlenberg. He continued in Virginia for a
time, organizing the local militias. On September 30, 1783, Congress
promoted him to major general. The army was then disbanded that
November.

Now a civilian, Muhlenberg moved back to Trappe and became an
original member of the Pennsylvania Society of the Cincinnati. In 1784,
he was elected to the Supreme Executive Council of the Commonwealth
of Pennsylvania. From 1785 to 1788, he was made Vice President of

Detail of Peter's grave

the Council (comparable to Lieutenant Governor). Muhlenberg resigned from this position on October 14, 1788.

Next, Muhlenberg was elected to the First Congress along with his brother Frederick who became the first Speaker of the House. In 1793, Muhlenberg founded the Democratic-Republican Societies and won seats as a Republican in the Third and Sixth Congresses.

Muhlenberg was elected by the Pennsylvania legislature to the U.S. Senate in February 1801, defeating George Logan. However, he resigned in June 1801 when President Thomas Jefferson appointed him as the supervisor for revenue in Pennsylvania. He was made customs collector for Philadelphia in 1802, a post he held until his death.

On August 3, 1805, Muhlenberg wrote a letter appealing to the mostly German residents of Berks and Northampton counties to convince them to vote for Governor Thomas McKean rather than the German Simon Snyder who was backed by a radical Democratic faction keen to upset the Constitution. McKean won, and the margin of victory could be found in those counties.

Peter Muhlenberg died on October 1, 1807, his 61st birthday, at Gray's Ferry, Pennsylvania. He was buried at the Augustus Lutheran Church in Trappe next to his father.

There is a memorial to Peter Muhlenberg on Connecticut Avenue in Washington, D.C. The inscription reads, "John Peter Gabriel Muhlenberg 1746–1807 Serving His Church, His Country, His State." Another memorial stands at the Philadelphia Museum of Art. Muhlenberg County, Kentucky is named after him.

Woodstock, Virginia is the home of two statues of Muhlenberg; one in front of the Shenandoah County Courthouse; the other at the Emmanuel Lutheran Church.

A statue of Peter Muhlenberg is located in front of the Shenandoah County Courthouse in Woodstock, Virginia. That town's Emmanuel Lutheran congregation preserves his communion vessels, a baptismal font, and an altar cloth.

Another statue of Peter Muhlenberg is located at Muhlenberg College in Allentown, Pennsylvania in front of the Haas College Center on Chew Street.

U.S. Congressman Francis Swaine Muhlenberg, a son of Peter Muhlenberg, represented Ohio for a term. A nephew, Henry Augustus Philip Muhlenberg, had a much longer career in the Congress and was the first United States Minister to the Austrian Empire. A great-great-grandson, Frederick Augustus Muhlenberg was a Representative and Senator from Pennsylvania.

Historian Jerome Greene recently wrote about Muhlenberg, "Outside his home state, he is not well known, but Muhlenberg was one of the many steady unsung heroes of the war."

Molly Pitcher (Mary Ludwig)
(1744 or 1754–1832)

Sergeant Molly

Buried at Old Graveyard,
Carlisle, Pennsylvania.

Revolutionary War Heroine

Molly Pitcher was a nickname given to a woman who fought in the Battle of Monmouth, during the American Revolutionary War. Her real name was Mary Ludwig. There is disagreement among scholars about several essential details of her life, beginning with her date of birth. Her cemetery marker indicates that she was born on October 13, 1744, but others point to evidence suggesting it may have been October 13, 1754. Her father is believed to have been a butcher (but may have been a dairy farmer). There is little doubt that Mary was raised as a hard worker. In 1768, she was sent to Carlisle, Pennsylvania, to become a servant in the home of Dr. William Irvine. The following year she married a local barber named William Hays.

Five years later, on July 12, 1774, in a meeting in the Presbyterian Church in Carlisle, Mary's employer (Dr. Irvine) organized a town boycott of British goods as a protest of the Tea Act of 1773. Mary's husband's name (William Hays) appears on a list of people who were charged with enforcing the boycott. In 1775, when the Revolutionary War began, William Hays enlisted in the Colonial Army.

After her husband's enlistment, Mary at first stayed in Carlisle. She then went to live with her parents near Philadelphia (so that she could be closer to her husband's regiment). During the winter of 1777, Mary

Molly Pitcher at the Battle of Monmouth

joined her husband at the Continental Army's winter camp at Valley Forge. She joined a group of "camp followers," who were led by Martha Washington. These women were of great importance to the army. As a general rule, women were not allowed to fight as soldiers. Instead, they cooked and washed the soldiers' clothes. They gathered and preserved food and supplies, and they repaired uniforms, blankets, and other items. They cared for the sick, wounded, and dying soldiers.

In the spring of 1778, the Continental Army was retrained under Baron von Steuben. During this time, William Hays trained as an artilleryman. Mary Hays and other camp followers served as "water girls" during the training, carrying water to drilling infantry troops. Artillerymen also needed a constant supply of water to cool down the hot cannon barrels and to soak the rag ("rammer rag") tied to the end of the ramrod with which they cleaned sparks and gunpowder out of the barrel after each shot.

The term "Molly Pitcher" was commonly used by Continental Army soldiers. It resulted from a combination of the name "Molly" (a widely-used nickname at the time for women named Mary or Margaret) and the term "pitcher" (the containers of water women carried on the battlefield).

The Battle of Monmouth took place on June 28, 1778, in modern-day Freehold, New Jersey. The Continental Army under General George Washington attacked the rear of the British Army column commanded by Lieutenant General Sir Henry Clinton as they left Monmouth Court House. With the temperature above 100 degrees that day, both sides lost almost as many men to heatstroke as to the enemy. It was during that battle that Mary Ludwig Hays earned the nickname "Molly Pitcher," becoming one of the most popular female images of the Revolutionary War.

Just before the battle started, Mary found a spring to serve as her water supply. (There are currently two different places within Monmouth Battlefield State Park that are marked as the "Molly Pitcher Spring.") She spent the early part of the day carrying water under heavy fire from British troops. Sometime during the battle, Mary saw her husband collapse either from heat exhaustion or because he was wounded (but regardless managed to survive). For the rest of the day, Mary stepped in and continued to "swab and load" the cannon using her husband's ramrod. She continued to do this until the battle was over. According to accounts, at one point, while loading a cartridge with her feet far apart, a British musket ball flew between her legs and took off the lower part of her petticoat. Mary supposedly said, "Well that could have been worse" and went back to swabbing and loading. Later that evening, the fighting stopped, and the British forces retreated and moved on. The Battle of Monmouth was seen as a significant victory for Americans.

Mary's legendary heroism was noted, and she was commissioned as a sergeant by General Greene (or by some accounts by George Washington himself). From that day forward, she was known as "Sergeant Molly." An old Revolutionary rhyme tells the story:

Moll Pitcher, she stood by her gun
And rammed the charges home, sir;
And thus on Monmouth bloody field
A sergeant did become, sir.

Until the close of the Revolutionary War, Molly Pitcher remained with the army and proved to be a beloved and valuable helping hand. After the war, she and her husband returned to Carlisle, and Mary went back to work as a domestic servant. In 1780, they had a son, John L. Hays. In 1786, William Hays died, and Mary married John McCauley, another veteran of the Revolutionary War. McCauley was a stone cutter. The marriage was reportedly not a happy one, and sometime between 1807 and 1810, John McCauley disappeared. It is not known what became of him.

Mary Ludwig Hays McCauley was known throughout Carlisle as Molly Pitcher. She lived in a house on the corner of North and Bedford Streets, which has since been demolished. In 1822, the state legislature awarded Molly Pitcher a sum of $40 and subsequent annual payments of $40 each "for the rest of her life."

On January 22, 1852, Mary died in Carlisle and was buried in the Old Graveyard with military honors. Her grave was unmarked, and her obituary did not mention her war contributions.

In 1856, Mary's son John L. Hays died. His obituary noted that he "was a son of the ever-to-be-remembered heroine, the celebrated 'Molly Pitcher' whose deeds of daring are recorded in the annals of the Revolution and over whose remains a monument ought to be erected."

On July 4, 1876, the 100th anniversary of the Declaration of Independence, the citizens of Carlisle erected a white marble monument over Mary's grave. It commemorates "Molly Pitcher, the heroine of Monmouth."

To complicate the story, there is another similar heroic story of a woman in the Revolutionary War. Margaret Corbin was the wife of John Corbin of Philadelphia, who was also an artilleryman in the Continental Army. On November 12, 1776, John Corbin was killed defending Fort Washington in northern Manhattan. Margaret took his place at his cannon and continued to fire it until she was wounded. In 1779, she was awarded an annual pension by the Continental Congress. She was the first woman in the United States to receive a military pension. She is buried at West Point. Her nickname was "Captain Molly."

Monument to Molly Pitcher

So the name "Molly Pitcher" comes down to us as a symbol of courage and resourcefulness under fire. The story of Molly Pitcher was told for many generations. It inspired women of her time and captured the hearts of America. In 1928, Molly Pitcher was honored with an overprint on a U.S. postage stamp reading "MOLLY PITCHER" in capital letters. In 1978, the 200th anniversary of the Battle of Monmouth, Molly was pictured on an imprinted stamp on a postal card. She was further honored in World War II with the naming of the Liberty Ship *SS Molly Pitcher*. On its maiden voyage, it was torpedoed on March 17, 1943, by a German U-Boat about 500 miles west of Lisbon, Spain.

The stretch of U.S. Route 11 between Shippensburg and the Pennsylvania-Maryland state line is known as the "Molly Pitcher Highway." There is a Molly Pitcher Ale House on 2nd Avenue and 85th Street in Manhattan, a Molly Pitcher Brewing Company in Atascadero, California, and a Molly Pitcher Inn in Red Bank, New Jersey, not far from the site of the Battle of Monmouth.

Statue of Molly Pitcher

Joseph Reed
(1741–1785)

President of Pennsylvania

Buried at Laurel Hill Cemetery,
Philadelphia, Pennsylvania.

————•◦•————

Military • Continental Congress • Articles of Confederation

Joseph Reed served in the Continental Congress and signed the Articles of Confederation. He was one of George Washington's aides-de-camp early in the Revolutionary War and held the ranks of colonel and adjutant-general. Given his background, money, education, and marriage, he was an unlikely revolutionist. He was an enigma to many as he at first believed that reconciliation with Britain was both desirable and possible. His reluctance to commit to the cause made him seem to be trying to be on the winning side for his gain. George Washington was a big supporter of Joseph Reed, but Reed even turned on Washington when things weren't looking very good for the general.

———⯈◦⯇———

Joseph Reed was born in Trenton, New Jersey on August 27, 1741. He was the son of Andrew Reed, a merchant, and Theodora Bowes. Reed's ancestors had come to America from Northern Ireland and were well established by the time Joseph was born. The family moved to Philadelphia from Trenton shortly after Joseph's birth, and he was enrolled at Philadelphia Academy. He received his bachelor's degree in 1757 at the age of sixteen from the College of New Jersey, which became

Joseph Reed

Princeton University. Soon after, he studied law under Richard Stockton the able, eloquent Princetonian who was acknowledged to be one of the best lawyers and who would become a signer of the Declaration of Independence. In 1763 Reed went to England to study law at the prestigious Middle Temple in London. He studied there for two years often attending debates in the House of Commons. During this time he met an Englishwoman named Esther deBerdt. They married in May of 1770. Reed returned to America with his wife and widowed mother-in-law in October of 1770. He set up a law practice in Trenton at first but soon moved to Philadelphia. There the couple had five children. Esther started an organization called the Daughters of Liberty, to raise money in support of the war. She died in September 1780, and Ben Franklin's daughter Sarah Bache took over the organization.

Reed focused on becoming a leading lawyer in Philadelphia and confronted suspicions that he was a Loyalist as he had marital and familial ties with the mother country. He slowly came to feel that independence was the only course for the colonies to take. In the two years before the war, he worked as a member of Philadelphia's Committee of Correspondence and as president of Pennsylvania's second Provincial Congress.

When the army was formed in April 1775, Reed became a lieutenant colonel. On June 19, 1775, four days after George Washington was elected commander in chief, he was asked to join Washington's staff. He joined Washington in Cambridge and was appointed as his secretary. Three months later, Reed departed, pleading the press of cases pending in his law practice. Washington requested that he return, but Reed was reluctant to do so. In March 1776, Washington offered him the job of Adjutant General, and he reluctantly accepted. He performed well and became one of Washington's most trusted officers. His judgment in military matters was consistently good and his advice to Washington excellent. However, to many, he seemed irresolute and wavering, wondering which current would become the mainstream.

After the loss of Fort Washington, the last outpost in colonial hands on Manhattan Island, Reed along with other generals, questioned Washington's judgments, especially allowing New York City to be dangerously open to invasion. Reed had not told Washington of his feelings but wrote to General Charles Lee, a letter that was a stunning criticism of Washington and praised Lee. Unhappily for all involved, when Reed was absent from headquarters, Washington opened a communication from Lee to Reed that indicated that they were both questioning Washington's abilities. This was extremely upsetting to Washington as Reed was one of his most trusted and relied upon officers. The aftermath was an awkwardness between the two that could not be repaired. The intimate relationship they had once was gone for good. Washington remained professional however and allowed Reed to continue. As a former resident of Trenton and Princeton, Reed knew that area well and supplied Washington with vital information before and during the battles of Trenton and Princeton. Three weeks after the victory at Princeton, Reed resigned as Adjutant General and then curiously volunteered as an aide without pay in time to serve at the battles of Brandywine, Germantown, and Monmouth.

In 1777, Reed was offered the positions of brigadier general and Chief Justice of the Supreme Court of Pennsylvania. He declined both in favor of being elected as a delegate to the Continental Congress. In 1778 he was one of five Pennsylvania delegates to sign the Articles of Confederation. Also that year he was elected to the equivalent position to Pennsylvania Governor, President of the Supreme Executive Council of Pennsylvania, with an almost unanimous vote. He was re-elected to this position twice. During his administration, he helped oversee the passage of a statute that abolished slavery in Pennsylvania. He also was successful in getting Revolutionary War soldiers placed on half-pay for life. Also during this time, he pressed charges against Benedict Arnold

The grave of Joseph Reed

for corruption and military malpractice while he was in command at Philadelphia. The subsequent court-martial largely exonerated Arnold, but his resentment over this matter is thought to have fueled his later traitorous behavior.

Also in 1778, he was caught up in a scandal in which he was accused of traitorous correspondence with England. Until his name was cleared long after his death, some people questioned his loyalty which may be why he took such a strong stance against Loyalists. He was very strongly anti-Loyalist, advocating in Congress for property seizure and treason charges against anyone who sympathized with the Crown. As President of Pennsylvania, Reed oversaw numerous trials of suspected Loyalists. After James Wilson defended 23 people accused of treason, a mob, stirred up by Reed's speeches, attacked Wilson in what was to become known as the "Battle of Fort Wilson." The arrival of militia saved Wilson and his friends after one casualty from inside Wilson's house. A number of the mob were arrested, but Reed pardoned and released them.

After Reed's term as President of Pennsylvania ended in 1781, he returned to practicing law. He was again elected to Congress in 1784 but declined to serve because of deteriorating health. Joseph Reed died at his house in Philadelphia on March 5, 1785. He was initially buried in the Arch Street Presbyterian Burial Grounds in Philadelphia but was removed to Laurel Hill when that cemetery was abolished in 1868.

David Rittenhouse
(1732–1796)

Scientist, Surveyor, and First Mint Director

Buried at Laurel Hill Cemetery,
Philadelphia, Pennsylvania.

***

Scientist • Surveyor • U.S. Mint

David Rittenhouse was an important figure at the founding of our nation. He was a friend of many of the founders in his role as a surveyor, clockmaker, astronomer, inventor, mathematician, and scientist. During the Revolutionary War, he served on the Council of Safety and in the Pennsylvania Constitution convention. He accurately surveyed many state boundaries and was a member of the American Philosophical Society with Ben Franklin. Rittenhouse was also the first director of the United States Mint and may be the reason we have stars on a field of blue on our flag.

***

David Rittenhouse was born April 8, 1732, near Germantown, Pennsylvania, then a separate village from Philadelphia. His parents, Matthias and Elizabeth Williams Rittenhouse, were farmers in a little village called Rittenhousetown in Roxborough Township, Philadelphia County. His father was of German Mennonite descent while his mother was Welsh Quaker; however, neither denomination was emphasized in the home.

William Rittenhouse, his great grandfather, had built the first paper mill in the British colonies in Germantown in 1690. When his uncle

David Rittenhouse

William, also a miller, died, David inherited his tools and instructional books from which he gained much of his early informal education. As a lad, young David was adept at building mechanical models and demonstrating mathematical skills. At only eight years of age, he made a model of a water mill.

Soon, at only 13 years of age, Rittenhouse acquired other books like Newton's *Principia*, which helped him master Newton's laws of motion and gravity. Rittenhouse began to construct clocks, making a wooden one when he was seventeen and one of brass soon after. By age 19, in 1751, he opened a shop on the road that ran by his father's farm where he sold clocks, mathematical instruments, and mechanical models of the solar system. This was in what is now East Norriton Township near the Valley Forge Medical Center and Hospital.

Rittenhouse became very skilled at constructing astronomical instruments by 1756, experimenting with telescopes and mechanical models. He made surveyors' compasses, levels, transits, and zenith sectors as well as thermometers, barometers, at least one hygrometer, and occasional eyeglasses. During 1763 to 1764, Rittenhouse surveyed the boundary between Pennsylvania and Delaware, measuring a 12-mile circle from the New Castle, Delaware courthouse. This measurement was so precise that it was included without modification into the work by Mason and Dixon for the Pennsylvania-Maryland border.

On February 20, 1766, Rittenhouse took time away from his tinkering to marry Eleanor Coulston with whom he eventually had two daughters: Elizabeth (born 1767) and Ester (born 1769).

In 1768, Rittenhouse was admitted as a member of the American Philosophical Society, eventually serving as librarian and secretary. After Ben Franklin's passing in 1790, Rittenhouse became vice president and then president until 1796. The Society thought Rittenhouse the perfect person to study the upcoming transit of Venus. Rittenhouse had built an observatory in his backyard having constructed his telescope. To observe the transit, he thought he needed 22 of them set up at various locations. The legislature funded this.

When the transit of Venus occurred on June 3, 1769, Rittenhouse and his team were ready to make their observations. Rittenhouse was so excited as he lay under his telescope that he momentarily fainted. He had been ill the week prior and was still weak, though he recovered to continue his work. Rittenhouse also noticed that Venus had an atmosphere, a fact that was not previously known. He also calculated the average distance between the earth and the sun at 93 million miles. The American Philosophical Society subsequently published the results of the transit though no mention was made of his fainting and the significance of the atmospheric finding was not recognized for over a century.

Due to his balky health, perhaps to a duodenal ulcer, Rittenhouse moved his family to Philadelphia permanently in 1770. Around this time, he built an advanced orrery (a scale model of the solar system) for the College of New Jersey (now Princeton). Later, he made a more advanced model that he gave to the College of Philadelphia (now the

University of Pennsylvania). Rittenhouse earned honorary degrees from both institutions, and the orreries still exist in their collections.

Tragically, Eleanor Rittenhouse died in 1771 at the age of 35 while in childbirth. The baby also did not survive. David remarried the following year Hannah Jacobs with whom he had no surviving children. Hannah lived until 1799 and may be the reason Rittenhouse was a Presbyterian later in life.

From 1773 and onward, it was Rittenhouse's astronomical obser-vations that were utilized by almanacs in Pennsylvania, Maryland, and Virginia.

During the American Revolution, Rittenhouse was the engineer and vice president of the Committee of Safety and served on the Board of War. Rittenhouse was concerned with the production of saltpeter and guns and helped to design the Delaware River defenses. He also experi-mented with telescopic sights for rifles and rifled cannon. Rittenhouse participated in the creation of the Pennsylvania Constitution of 1776. He was then the treasurer of Pennsylvania from 1777 to 1789.

Francis Hopkinson, a close friend and colleague who was on the Navy Board, wrote the Flag Act of 1777 in which he explained the blue field of stars as a "new constellation." Some attribute this thought to Rittenhouse.

Amid the tensions with Britain, Rittenhouse also continued his aca-demic work. From 1779 to 1782 he was a Professor of Astronomy at what is now the University of Pennsylvania. He was subsequently vice-provost of the university from 1780 to 1782 and trustee from 1782 until his death. In 1781, he was the first American to spot the planet Uranus. The next year he was elected a Fellow of the American Academy of Arts and Sciences.

Rittenhouse's first work with coinage was regarding the Nova Constellatio (New Constellation) pattern coins which were minted in Philadelphia in 1783 at the behest of Robert Morris. Rittenhouse was consulted on the design which resembles the stars on the flag.

In 1784, Rittenhouse and Andrew Ellicott finished the Mason-Dixon line to the southwest corner of Pennsylvania. This was the last of his survey-ing work. Previously, he had also helped locate other boundaries between

In
Memory of
DAVID RITTENHOUSE
born April 8th 1732
died June 26th 1796
Also
HANNAH RITTENHOUSE
his Wife
who died October 15th 1799
Aged 64 years.

The grave of Rittenhouse

Pennsylvania, New York, New Jersey, and the Northwest Territory. He also worked on borders for Massachusetts.

In 1786, next to the octagonal observatory he had built previously, Rittenhouse constructed a new Georgian-style house at 4th and Arch Streets in Philadelphia. Every Wednesday he held a salon meeting with such luminaries as Ben Franklin, Francis Hopkinson, Pierre Eugene du Simitiere, Thomas Jefferson (when in town), and others. Jefferson once wrote he would rather attend one of these meetings "than spend a whole week in Paris." In his *Notes on the State of Virginia* published a few years prior Jefferson listed Rittenhouse, Franklin, and Washington as examples of New World genius when refuting French naturalist Georges-Louis Leclerc, Comte de Buffon's claim that the intellects of the people living there were stunted by the environment and climate of North America.

During the Washington administration, the need for a national coinage came to the forefront. Rittenhouse was selected the first Director of the Mint, and set about to issue coins, opening the first mint on April 2, 1792. On the morning of July 30, 1792, Washington provided the silver flatware himself that was melted to become the first coin planchettes. Rittenhouse then personally tested the equipment, hand striking the first coins which were given to Washington in appreciation of his many contributions. Coin production on a large scale was begun in 1793. Rittenhouse remained the Mint Director until June 30, 1795, when he resigned due to declining health.

In his later years, Rittenhouse founded the Democratic-Republican Societies in Philadelphia in 1793. In 1795, he was honored to become a member of the Royal Society of London, a rare recognition for an American scientist.

David Rittenhouse died at his home on June 26, 1796. He is now buried at Laurel Hill Cemetery in Philadelphia.

There are several tributes to David Rittenhouse:

- There is a crater on the moon named Rittenhouse Crater.
- In 1825, Southwest Square in Philadelphia was renamed Rittenhouse Square.
- The University of Pennsylvania has the David Rittenhouse Laboratory.
- The David Rittenhouse Junior High School is in Norristown, Pennsylvania.

Betsy Ross
(1752–1836)

American Seamstress

Buried at Betsy Ross House Grounds,
Philadelphia, Pennsylvania.

———•◆•———

Legendary Patriot Figure

———◆◆◆———

This founder's grandson, William Canby, wrote about her association with the American flag in the 1870s. According to Canby, his account was based on conversations with family members, including his grandmother. In a speech to the Historical Society of Pennsylvania, he spoke of a visit made by George Washington and two members of the Continental Congress to a seamstress shop on Arch Street in Philadelphia. Their purpose was to create a flag proclaiming the independence of the United States. They met with the seamstress and showed her a rough sketch of what they had in mind. The four talked over ideas and agreed on a rectangular banner of red, white, and blue distinguished by an unusual field of five-pointed stars. The woman was an enterprising Quaker who would produce the first American flag and distinguish herself as one of just a handful of Revolutionary heroines. Her name was Betsy Ross.

———◆◆◆———

Ross was born on January 1, 1752, in Philadelphia as Elizabeth Griscom. "Betsy" was the eighth of seventeen children and one of nine that survived childhood. She grew up in a strict Quaker household and was educated at a Quaker-run state school. It was an aunt who taught her

Betsy Ross

the art of sewing—a skill that would lead to the part she played in the history of the United States of America.

In 1773 the then Betsy Griscom eloped and married John Ross, the nephew of, George Ross, a future signer of the Declaration of Independence and the son of an Episcopal minister. As a result of the marriage, she was expelled from the Quaker congregation. The union also resulted in a split in the Griscom family. The young couple started their own upholstery business and joined the city-parish of Christ Church. On occasion, their worship services were joined by a Virginia militia commander by the name of George Washington.

When the American Revolution began, John Ross was a member of the Pennsylvania Provincial Militia and was assigned to guard munitions. He passed away in 1775. Some claim his death came as a result of an explosion involving gunpowder though this has never been verified. After his death, his wife stayed busy in the upholstery business working on uniforms and tents to help supply the Continental Army. She was also known to be one of several flag makers in Philadelphia

Ross would marry twice more in her lifetime. Her second husband was a mariner whose ship was captured by the British. Charged with treason, he was imprisoned in England where he died. Her third husband had met her second husband in jail and brought her the news of his death. These three marriages produced seven daughters, five of whom survived childhood.

Ross worked as a seamstress until her retirement in 1827. She spent her final years in the care of one of her daughters. She passed away on January 30, 1836, at the age of 84. She was initially buried in the Free Quaker Burial Ground in Philadelphia. Twenty years later her remains were moved to the Mt. Moriah Cemetery in Philadelphia. In 1875 as part of the coming American Centennial celebration, the city fathers decided to remove her remains to the Betsy Ross House where she was believed to have resided. Workers found no remains under her tombstone. There were other bones found in the family plot that were deemed to be hers. These bones were buried in the tomb at the Betsy Ross House—a tourist attraction that attracts thousands of visitors each year.

There is no doubt that Ross was hired to make flags for the American Navy during the Revolution. Records of the Pennsylvania Navy Board includes orders to pay her for this work. Historians have disputed the account made by William Canby holding that his story is unsubstantiated and that it came at a time when Americans were eager for tales highlighting the heroes and heroines of the struggle for American Independence. A history buff by the name of Robert Morris spent five years investigating the story. He concluded that while Ross didn't design the flag, she did suggest some changes to the design made by Francis Hopkinson and presented to her by Washington. Morris believes that Ross suggested that the flag's stars be five-pointed rather than six-pointed. He also believes that it was Ross who proposed that the flag be a rectangle rather than a square. As a result of his work, Morris came to believe that Ross was a hardworking, patriotic woman who played a noteworthy role in American history. He also believes that on the recommendation of George Ross, her first husband's uncle, Congress decided to have Betsy Ross sew the first the American flag.

The Betsy Ross Bridge that connects Philadelphia with Pennsauken Township, New Jersey is named in her honor. In 1952 the United States Post Office issued a commemorative stamp showing her presenting the completed flag to George Washington with Robert Morris and George Ross present at the event. Biographer Maria Miller wrote that in her opinion Ross is representative of more than a single flag. Instead, her story reflects and is a symbol of the lives of many working men and women who contributed to the cause of independence.

The grave of Betsy Ross

George Ross
(1730–1779)

Lawyer, Colonel, and Congressman

Buried at Christ Church Burial Ground,
Philadelphia, Pennsylvania.

Continental Association • Declaration of Independence

George Ross was a founder from Pennsylvania who was a signer of the Continental Association (1774) and the Declaration of Independence (1776). He served as a Judge of the Admiralty Court of Pennsylvania, a colonel in the Continental Army and Vice-President of the Pennsylvania Constitutional Convention.

George Ross was born to a man of the same name and Catherine Van Gezel in New Castle, Delaware on May 10, 1730. George Sr. was an Episcopal Church clergyman. George Jr. received his education at home and went on to study law at the age of 18 under the supervision of his older brother, who had a law practice in Philadelphia. In 1750, after only two years of study, he was admitted to the Pennsylvania bar at the age of 20. The next year Ross set up his law practice in Lancaster, Pennsylvania and soon married one of his first clients, Anne Lawler. The couple would have a daughter and two sons.

He practiced law for several years and attained a good reputation. In 1756, Ross was chosen to be the Crown Prosecutor. At that time he was a Tory and loyal to the King. Ross served in that position for twelve

George Ross

years and in 1768 was elected to the provisional legislature. It was while serving there that he was able to better understand the colonial struggle against the Crown and its taxation policies, and he began to change his views.

He often opposed the Royal Governor, and while he had opposed American independence, in 1774, he changed his mind and began to support the patriot cause. As his passion for the patriot cause grew and became known, Ross was elected to the Continental Congress, receiving more popular votes than anyone except Ben Franklin. He served on the Committee of Safety overseeing the defense of the colonies.

In 1776 he was re-elected to the Continental Congress, appointed a colonel in the Continental Army, and was vice president of the State Constitutional Convention where he helped draft the Pennsylvania Bill of Rights. However, he stopped short of signing the controversial

Pennsylvania Constitution of 1776, ending the rule of the Penn family and establishing Pennsylvania as an independent commonwealth. Ross believed the constitution was too radical. That same year he joined the Continental Congress after the historic vote for independence but was present on August 2 for the signing. He was the last of the Pennsylvania delegation to affix his signature.

He was re-elected to the Congress again in 1777 but resigned that same year because of poor health. He would not be out of public service for long however as in 1778, he was elected Vice President of the Pennsylvania Assembly, and he accepted a judgeship in the Pennsylvania Court of Admiralty. While serving on the court, he was involved in the controversial decision regarding *United States vs. Peters*. A congressional court of appeals overruled his decision in the case involving a dispute between a sailor from Connecticut, Gideon Olmstead, and the state of Pennsylvania regarding the spoils from a captured ship, the British sloop *Active*. Olmstead was among a group of captive American sailors who overtook the sloop while they were being pressed into service. The sloop was then captured by American privateers who planned to sell the ship for a profit. The higher court ruled the captured sailors deserved a share,

The grave of George Ross

but the Pennsylvania Court disagreed. Ross refused to acknowledge the authority of the higher court to counter state decisions because a jury had been involved.

Perhaps Ross's most famous contribution to the new nation was not his alone. George had a niece, Betsy Ross (born Elizabeth Phoebe Griscom in 1752). She acquired her famous last name when she married Ross's nephew, John Ross. John and Betsy had a sewing business in Philadelphia, and Betsy was an excellent seamstress. The story told by Betsy's descendants was that one day in May of 1776, a three-member committee from the Continental Congress came to call upon her. Those representatives, General George Washington, Robert Morris, and George Ross, asked her to sew the first American flag based on a design Washington had drafted. The stars and stripes created by Ross would eventually be officially adopted by the Congress on June 14, 1777, as the official banner of the new nation.

Unfortunately, in 1779, at the age of 49, George Ross died from a violent attack of gout and didn't live to see independence. On his deathbed, Ross said that he was sure he was going to a place where "there were the most excellent wines." He was buried at Christ Church in Philadelphia.

Benjamin Rush
(1745–1813)

The Doctor in the House

Buried at Christ Church Burial Ground,
Philadelphia, Pennsylvania.

———•◦•———

Declaration of Independence

By the age of thirty this founder was already a prominent Philadelphia physician. In time he would be recognized as the most outstanding physician of his day. He is regarded as the father of American psychiatry. He founded Dickinson College and is one of the founders of Franklin and Marshall College. He also found the time to work as a leader for social and political reforms. He served in the Continental Congress and signed the Declaration of Independence. He was the surgeon general of the middle department of the Continental Army. During the ratification fight over the United States Constitution he championed the Federalist cause in Pennsylvania. In 1799 President John Adams appointed him to the position of Treasurer of the United States Mint. This accomplished founder's name was Benjamin Rush.

———◦◦◦———

Rush was born on Christmas Eve in 1745 near the city of Philadelphia. His father was a farmer and a gunsmith who passed away when his son was five years of age. His mother sent the boy to Maryland where he was raised by his uncle, Samuel Finley, who ran the West Nottingham Academy, a private school. It was his uncle who encouraged Rush to become a doctor. Rush first attended medical school at the College of

Benjamin Rush

Philadelphia and then travelled to England where he obtained his medical degree from the University of Edinburgh in 1768. A year later Rush returned to America and opened a medical practice in Philadelphia. He also taught chemistry at the College of Philadelphia where he wrote the first American text on chemistry.

In addition to practicing medicine, Rush wholeheartedly threw himself into the political turmoil brewing between England and the American colonies. He joined the Sons of Liberty and began writing essays advocating American independence. His political activities led to his appointment to the Second Continental Congress in 1776. He took his seat on July 20th which meant he had missed the chance to vote in favor of the Declaration of Independence but on August 2, 1776 he became one of the youngest signers of that document. Years later he described that moment in a letter to his good friend John Adams. Rush wrote, "Do you recollect the pensive and awful silence which pervaded the house when we were called up one after another, to the table of the President of

Congress to subscribe what was believed by many at that time to be our own death warrants?"

The year 1776 was indeed a momentous one for Rush. In addition to signing the Declaration he was wed that January. The bride was the 17-year-old Julia Stockton who happened to be the daughter of Richard Stockton of Princeton, New Jersey. Thus, Julia Stockton became unique as both the daughter and wife of a signer of the Declaration of Independence.

Rush was friends with the writer Thomas Paine and he encouraged Paine to publish the work *Common Sense*. Rush suggested the title for the politically influential piece which was a major factor in mobilizing colonial resistance to British rule. Rush was said to be relieved that there was someone beside himself who was willing to compose such an anti-British tract. Rush shared the sentiments expressed in Paine's work but feared that had he been the one to express them it would damage his image in Philadelphia.

In April of 1777, Rush was commissioned Surgeon General of the Middle Department of the Continental Army. Almost immediately Rush found himself in conflict with Dr. William Shippen, Jr., the director general of hospitals for the army. He blamed Shippen for the poor health conditions he witnessed in his new position. It is not an overstatement to say he was horrified by the health conditions that plagued the Continental Army. He then put these criticisms in writing. General Washington referred the matter to Congress which investigated and then dismissed the charges.

Rush had also written several letters critical of General Washington. In 1778 he sent a letter anonymously to the governor of Virginia, Patrick Henry. In the missive Rush expressed the view that the army would be better served if Washington was removed from command and replaced with Horatio Gates, Charles Lee, or Thomas Conway. The letter made its way to Washington who recognized the handwriting. Rush himself recognized that, as a result, the handwriting was on the wall and he resigned from the army and resumed his medical practice.

After the 1787 convention produced the Constitution, Rush became a strong proponent in favor of its ratification. He addressed Pennsylvania's ratifying convention saying that, "the hand of God was employed in this work, as that God had divided the Red Sea to give passage to the children of Israel." When the Constitution was ratified by the necessary number of states he proclaimed that it was, "as much the work of divine providence as any of the miracles recorded in the Old and New Testament were the effects of a divine power." Rush viewed the ratification as a sign that the heavens favored the Federalist side of the question.

In 1793 a yellow fever epidemic hit Philadelphia that killed at least 5,000 people. Rush worked tirelessly during this period often treating 100 patients in a single day. His methods which included bloodletting and purging were controversial but the work he performed made him a local hero. He had his critics who claimed his methods killed as many people as they saved. That said few could question his humanitarian efforts. He treated many patients for no charge and he established the first free medical clinic in America.

In 1799 President John Adams appointed Rush to the position of Treasurer of the United States Mint. It was a job he held until his death in 1813. He was laid to rest in the Christ Church Burial Ground in Philadelphia.

Rush left behind a legacy of social and political reforms. He had served as the President of the Pennsylvania Society for Promoting the Abolition of Slavery. He sided with and led reform movements aimed at eliminating public punishment and capital punishment. He advocated for a property tax to support public education. His was a life lived well in service to both the public and his nation.

The grave of Benjamin Rush

Arthur St. Clair
(1737–1818)

First Governor of the Northwest Territory

Buried at Saint Clair Park Path,
Greensburg, Pennsylvania.

Military • President of Congress
First Governor of Northwest Territory

Arthur St. Clair, originally from Thurso, Scotland, was a political and military leader during the American Revolution and the first governor of the Northwest Territory in 1788 that later became Ohio, Indiana, Illinois, Michigan, and parts of Wisconsin and Minnesota.

St. Clair was a delegate to the Continental Congress who became its second to last President. He was also a major general in the Continental Army before losing his command following a retreat from Fort Ticonderoga. Later, in 1791, he was in command when American forces experienced their worst defeat by the Native Americans.

Historian Joseph J. Thompson called him "one of the most unique figures in American history . . . the handsome, polished, accomplished, profound St. Clair. The appearance and conduct of the men we have been considering were influenced by their rugged and rustic surroundings, but St. Clair was the product of culture and fashion."

Arthur St. Clair was born in Thurso, county of Caithness, Scotland in the 1730s. Some have estimated his birth year as 1734, but subsequent research points to March 23, 1736, as a reasonable date, which is 1737

Arthur St. Clair

on the modern calendar. The names of his parents are unknown, though one biographer states they were "probably" William Sinclair, a merchant, and Elizabeth (née Balfour or Hamilton).

It is believed St. Clair attended the University of Edinburgh for a time but then left to study anatomy with Dr. William Hunter, a leading Scottish physician, around 1756. Soon after, he quit and purchased a commission in the British army as an ensign and served in North America during the French and Indian War.

During the war, he served under General Jeffrey Amherst at the capture of Louisburg, Nova Scotia in July 1758. The following spring, he was promoted to lieutenant and served under General James Wolfe at the Battle of the Plains of Abraham resulting in the capture of Quebec City.

After the battle, St. Clair went on leave in Boston where he met his future wife, Phoebe Bayard, the niece of Governor James Bowdoin of Massachusetts colony. St. Clair married her, resigned his commission, and decided to settle in the Ligonier Valley near modern-day Pittsburgh, Pennsylvania using funds from his father-in-law. There he invested in mills and took a position as a surveyor, becoming the largest landowner in the region. Despite not being a lawyer, he was named a local justice and in a 1774 almanac was listed as a prothonotary in Bedford and Westmoreland Counties.

St. Clair was a proponent of Pennsylvania in its disputes with Virginia regarding the Ohio Country and Fort Pitt area. St. Clair worked with the natives in the area to promote the fur trade rather than see them give up their lands to the Virginians. Lord Dunmore's War ultimately settled the boundaries between the settlers and the natives at the Ohio River. St. Clair's actions likely spared the settlers in the Fort Pitt area from native vengeance.

At the outset of the American Revolution, St. Clair was a supporter of the patriot cause. He served on his local Committee of Safety and was the secretary to the representatives from the Continental Congress who negotiated with the Indians of the Ohio Country. In 1775, the Congress appointed him as a colonel in the 3rd Pennsylvania Regiment of the Continental Army and he participated in the attack on Canada at the Battle of Trois-Rivières. Afterward, he was appointed to brigadier general and in August 1776 was sent by Washington to organize the New Jersey militia. During the winter of 1776-77, he was with Washington at the battles of Trenton and Princeton. He crossed the Delaware River with Washington on the night of December 25-26, 1776, and many biographers credit him with the strategy that led to the capture of Princeton. He was promoted to major general in February 1777.

In the spring of 1777, St. Clair was assigned to command Fort Ticonderoga in New York. When the British invaded, knowing he could not hold the fort without heavy casualties, St. Clair abandoned the fort and retreated. George Washington was disappointed he left without a fight. A subsequent court-martial headed by General Benjamin Lincoln, however, found St. Clair innocent of all charges. Despite his exoneration, St. Clair was not given significant commands for the remainder of the war though he was an aide-de-camp to General Washington, who retained a high opinion of him. St. Clair was at Cornwallis's surrender at Yorktown.

After the Revolution, St. Clair was elected to the Continental Congress, serving from November 2, 1785, to November 28, 1787. During his last year in Congress, St. Clair was elected President of

Congress, succeeding Nathaniel Gorham, on February 2, 1787, amid Shay's Rebellion. After the rebellion was put down, the Congress passed the Northwest Ordinance, creating the Northwest Territory (comprising modern-day Ohio, Indiana, Illinois, Michigan, most of Wisconsin, and eastern Minnesota), and assigned St. Clair as the governor. His presidency ended on October 29, 1787, when he took over his new duties.

St. Clair named Cincinnati, Ohio, after the Society of Cincinnati, and made his headquarters there. He formulated Maxwell's Code, named after its printer, as the first written laws in the territory. In 1789, he convinced certain Indians in the area to give up their land claims by signing the Treaty of Fort Harmar. Several chiefs had refused to participate or sign the treaty triggering the Northwest Indian War or Little Turtle's War. St. Clair, proceeded to build forts in western Ohio. He sent General Josiah Harmar and 1500 troops to suppress the Indians, ordering them to destroy the village of the Miami at present-day Fort Wayne, Indiana. Shawnee chief Blue Jacket and Miami chief Little Turtle defeated Harmar's men in October 1790 in what is known as Harmar's Defeat. Harmar retreated to Fort Washington, present-day Cincinnati, and St. Clair then took up command personally.

On March 21, 1791, Secretary of War Henry Knox ordered St. Clair to establish a strong and permanent military presence in the region. Congress commissioned St. Clair to lead two 300-man regiments of regular troops and 1400 ill-trained militiamen to move against the main Miami town, Kekionga.

St. Clair and his men left Fort Washington on September 17. The men marched twenty miles in two days and then built Fort Hamilton. They then advanced forty-five miles northward, where they erected Fort Jefferson. Leading primarily untrained militiamen, St. Clair faced problems with desertion from the beginning of his campaign. Although it was still early fall, his men faced cold temperatures, rain, and snowfall. Due to the scarcity of supplies, many of the men became demoralized. Despite these problems, St. Clair continued to advance against the Miami (in what is present-day Indiana). By November 3, his men had arrived on the banks of the Wabash River, near some of the Miami villages. Little Turtle, Blue Jacket, and Tecumseh, aided by British collaborators Alexander McKee and Simon Girty, surprised the poorly-prepared

Americans at Fort Recovery, Ohio, near the headwaters of the Wabash River, with 2000 warriors on November 4, 1791.

Many of the poorly-trained American militiamen immediately fled. St. Clair led the regular soldiers in a bayonet charge and had two horses shot out from under him. Several bullets passed through his clothing, and one took off a lock of his hair.

The natives surrounded the American camp. After three hours of fighting—the remaining Americans fought through the natives as they began a long retreat. The survivors reached Fort Jefferson late that afternoon and evening but with limited quantities of food and supplies there, St. Clair ordered his forces to Fort Washington.

More than half of the Americans were killed or wounded, and the survivors haphazardly fled back to Fort Washington. The battle has since been known as St. Clair's Defeat, the Battle of the Wabash, the Columbia Massacre, or the Battle of a Thousand Slain. It was the most significant defeat of the U.S. Army by natives in American history. Only about fifty natives were killed. St. Clair was among the wounded. One of the survivors stated, "The ground was literally covered with the dead."

A subsequent investigation exonerated St. Clair, but he resigned his army commission in March 1792 at the request of President Washington. However, he continued to serve as the Governor of the Northwest Territory. Eventually, American forces led by General Anthony Wayne won the campaign, overwhelming the natives and resulting in the Treaty of Greenville in 1795.

St. Clair was a Federalist. He hoped to see two states created from the Ohio Territory to increase Federalist power. However, the Democratic-Republicans led by Thomas Jefferson continued to gain influence in the capital and the territory. Despite St. Clair's resistance, the U.S. Congress sanctioned the Enabling Act of 1802 which gave Ohioans the right to form a constitutional convention on the path to statehood. St. Clair remarked the U.S. Congress had no power to interfere in the affairs of those in the Ohio Territory. He also stated the people of the territory "are no more bound by an act of Congress than we would be bound by an edict of the first consul of France." This led to Jefferson removing St. Clair as territorial governor and prevented him from playing a role in organizing the state of Ohio in 1803.

The grave of Arthur St. Clair

Following his resignation as governor, St. Clair returned to Pennsylvania where he invested in iron mines in the Pittsburgh area and established a foundry to make stoves and castings. He was very liberal with his money, loaning it to friends and family.

Though Congress did pay him a pension of two thousand dollars on May 1, 1810, it was not enough to save St. Clair from financial trouble. He lost his vast landholdings and eventually moved into a small log cabin on the property of his daughter, Louisa St. Clair Robb, on a ridge between Ligonier and Greensburg. He died there on August 31, 1818.

St. Clair was buried in the Old Greensburg Cemetery which later became St. Clair Park in Greensburg, Pennsylvania. His wife Phoebe died shortly after and was buried next to him. A Masonic monument was later placed over their graves. Said the *National Intelligencer* newspaper at the time, "On the summit of the Chestnut Ridge which overlooks the valley of Ligonier, in which the commencement of the revolution found him in prosper; on this lonesome spot, exposed to winter winds, as cold and desolating as the tardy gratitude of his country, died Major General Arthur St. Clair. The traveler as he passed the place, was reminded of the celebrated Roman exile's reply, 'tell the citizens of Rome that you saw Caius Marius sitting amongst the ruins of Carthage.'"

St. Clair remained a controversial figure for years to come, his reputation attached to the defeat on the Wabash. This historian wonders if his reputation would have been different had George Washington lived longer and been able to remind everyone of St. Clair's contributions at Trenton and Princeton.

Arthur St. Clair has been honored in many ways:

- A portion of the Hermitage, St. Clair's home in Oak Grove, Pennsylvania (north of Ligonier), was later moved to Ligonier, Pennsylvania, where it is now preserved, along with St. Clair artifacts and memorabilia at the Fort Ligonier Museum.
- An American Civil War steamer was named USS *St. Clair*.
- The following places were named after him: Upper St. Clair, Pennsylvania; St. Clairsville, Pennsylvania; St. Clair, Schuylkill County, Pennsylvania; St. Clair Township, Westmoreland County, Pennsylvania; East St. Clair Township, Bedford County, Pennsylvania; West St. Clair Township, Bedford County, Pennsylvania; the St. Clair neighborhood in Pittsburgh, Pennsylvania; St. Clair Hospital, Mt. Lebanon, Pennsylvania; St. Clair Township in Butler County, Ohio; St. Clair Township in Columbiana County, Ohio; St. Clairsville, Ohio; St. Clair Avenue in Cleveland, Ohio; Fort St. Clair in Eaton, Ohio; St. Clair County, Illinois; St. Clair County, Missouri; St. Clair County, Alabama; St. Clair Street in Frankfort, Kentucky; and the three-star St. Clair Hotel in Sinclair St., Thurso, Caithness.

James Smith
(1719–1806)

York's Radical Revolutionary

Buried at First Presbyterian Memorial Gardens,
York, Pennsylvania.

———————

Declaration of Independence • Continental Congress

James Smith organized a volunteer company of militia in York County. It was the first volunteer company raised to oppose the British, and he was among the first of colonial leaders to call for a continental congress to discuss the problems with the home country. He served as a delegate from Pennsylvania to the first and second Continental Congresses and signed the historic Declaration of Independence.

———————

Exactly when James Smith was born is open to question. He was born in Ulster, Northern Ireland but would never admit to the year. In 1805 a fire destroyed his office and all his official papers. We know the family emigrated to America in 1727 and that James was a young boy. They settled in Chester County, Pennsylvania and James' father John died in 1761.

Young James was tutored in the classical education of the day by local clergy and attended the Philadelphia Academy (later known as the University of Pennsylvania). There he came to study under the distinguished provost Dr. Allison. He studied Latin and Greek and excelled at the art of surveying, which at that time was of great importance.

James Smith

When he completed his studies at the Philadelphia Academy, he decided to study law under his brother George and in the office of Thomas Cookson in Lancaster, Pennsylvania. He was admitted to the Pennsylvania Bar in 1745 and began a practice in Shippensburg, Pennsylvania but soon moved the practice to the flourishing town of York, Pennsylvania.

In 1760 at the age of 41, Smith married a woman from New Castle, Delaware, Eleanor Armor. They would have five children, four of whom would die without having children. James Smith has no living descendants.

Smith early perceived the gathering storm and was among the first Pennsylvanians to speak out fearlessly on the side of the patriots from Massachusetts and Virginia. In 1774 he attended a provincial assembly where he presented a paper he had written entitled "Essay on The

Constitutional Power of Great Britain Over The Colonies In America." In that paper, Smith recommends that the colonies boycott all British goods. He felt that such action would pressure the British Parliament to back away from some of their oppressive laws.

Later that same year, Smith organized a volunteer militia company in York which elected him captain. It was the first volunteer corps raised in Pennsylvania. In soon increased in size to a regiment and he was appointed its colonel, a title which in respect to him was honorary, sine he never assumed actual command.

The grave of James Smith

Emerging as one of the regions radical leaders, he was elected a delegate to the state convention in Philadelphia in January 1775. He concurred in the spirited declaration of that convention that "if the British administration should determine by force to effect a submission to the late arbitrary acts of the British Parliament, in such a situation, we hold it our indispensable duty to resist such force, and at every hazard to defend the rights of liberties of America." These were strong words considering that many Pennsylvanians hoped for some form of "accommodation" with the mother country. Also, in Pennsylvania, many of the delegates and citizens were Quakers and against any violence.

Smith did not take part in the debates in the Continental Congress that led to independence. He was added to Pennsylvania's delegation on July 20, 1776, by a provincial convention in time to sign the Declaration of Independence on August 2, 1776. On the evening of August sixth, he rode off to York with a printed broadside copy to read to the public in the town square.

Smith continued to serve in Congress and the state assembly through 1778. He lent his law office in York to the Board of War in 1777 when Congress had to flee Philadelphia and move operations there. He was elected a Brigadier General of the state militia in 1781 and resumed his law practice when the war ended.

In 1785, Smith was elected to Congress again but declined to serve because of his age. He never said how old he was and any legal papers that might have shed light on his age were destroyed in the aforementioned fire about a year before his death. Smith died on July 11, 1806, and was buried in the First Presbyterian Memorial Gardens in York, Pennsylvania. His grave marker says he was ninety-three.

Jonathan Bayard Smith
(1742–1812)

Quaker Educator

Buried at Mount Vernon Cemetery,
Philadelphia, Pennsylvania.

Military • Articles of Confederation

This founder was a native Pennsylvanian born and bred in Philadelphia. A graduate of Princeton, he entered the mercantile business owned and operated by his father. An ardent patriot he embraced the at times unpopular stance, especially among Quaker Pennsylvania, of taking up arms against the British. Elected to the Continental Congress, he endorsed and signed the Articles of Confederation. He was a great promoter of education in the new nation. His name was Jonathan Bayard Smith.

Smith was born on February 21, 1742. His father Samuel Smith moved to Philadelphia from New Hampshire. Once settled in Pennsylvania he opened a business and quickly became a prosperous and respected merchant. The elder Smith saw to it that his son received a quality education. In 1760 he graduated from Princeton, a university he would later serve as a trustee. It may have been his father who instilled in Smith his devotion to education that he exhibited throughout his life.

By 1775 Smith was already supporting independence for the American colonies. That same year he was elected secretary of the committee of public safety. An election to the Continental Congress followed

Jonathan Bayard Smith

in 1777. He served in Congress until November of 1778 and signed the Articles of Confederation on behalf of Pennsylvania. The Articles were finally ratified in 1781which for the first time formally formed the states into a union.

During this same time, he put his money where his mouth was. On December 1, 1777, Smith presided at a public meeting in Philadelphia where it was resolved, "That it be recommended to the council of safety that in this great emergency . . . every person between the age of 16 and 50 be ordered out under arms." Smith joined the militia becoming a lieutenant colonel in John Bayard's regiment. His commanding officer was his brother- in- law. It was after marrying Susannah Bayard that Smith took his wife's maiden name as his middle name.

After leaving Congress, Smith returned to running his business though he remained active in civic affairs. He promoted education and in 1779 was one of the founders of the University of the State of

Pennsylvania. In 1795 when it merged with two other schools to form the University of Pennsylvania Smith became a trustee—a position he would hold until his death. He also put in thirty years of service as a trustee at his alma mater, Princeton.

He remained active almost to his last days. When the War of 1812 broke out public meetings were held in Philadelphia sponsored by the Democratic Young Men, but it was the 70-year-old Smith who headed these meetings as the organization's president. He passed away on June 16, 1812, and was laid to rest with Masonic honors in the Cemetery of the Second Presbyterian Church. When that cemetery closed in 1867 Smith's was one of the approximately 2,500 graves moved to the Mount Vernon Cemetery where he now rests behind locked gates. We were unable to visit his grave because the cemetery, though still in operation, is not open to the public, has suffered from neglect and is widely overgrown. It is our understanding that local volunteers are looking at taking action to clean up what was once, and could be again a beautiful cemetery.

The locked gateway to Mount Vernon Cemetery, Philadelphia

Haym Solomon
(1740–1785)

Financier of the Revolutionary War

Buried at Mikveh Israel Cemetery,
Philadelphia, Pennsylvania.

———•••———

Financier

When this man was born on April 7, 1740, in Poland no one would have predicted that he would one day be considered a founder of a new nation. Yet this man from a Sephardic Jewish family came to the new world where he made his fortune. He then actively supported the patriot cause. While aiding Robert Morris, he became the man who may well have been the prime financier of the American side during the Revolution. All this came at considerable risk for he was captured by the British and only avoided a death sentence by escaping. He remains one of the lesser-known founders but one to whom this country owes much, perhaps independence itself. His name was Haym Solomon.

———✦✦✦———

Solomon was descendent of Spanish and Portuguese Jews who migrated to Poland after Ferdinand and Isabella expelled the Jews in those regions in the same year Columbus found his way to America. Solomon left Poland while still young, and during his travels, in Western Europe, he studied finance and became fluent in eight languages including German. His mastery of the German language would serve both him and the patriot cause well during the Revolution.

Haym Salomon

Solomon arrived in America in 1772 and settled in New York where his financial knowledge allowed him to start a business and become active as a dealer in foreign securities. He developed a strong friendship with Alexander McDougal, who was a wealthy and powerful man of Scottish descent known to be a leader against British rule. His relationship with McDougal resulted in his embrace of the Patriot cause, and soon Solomon became an active member in New York's Sons of Liberty. On September 20, 1776, a fire broke out in New York that destroyed 493 homes many of which the British had intended to use to house its troops. The English authorities blamed the sons for the fire and began to arrest the known members arbitrarily. Solomon was among those who were arrested by the English authorities accused of setting the fire.

Facing brutal prison conditions aboard an English ship, Solomon utilized his German. He showed the English he could converse with the Hessian soldiers who had been contracted by King George III. He worked as an interpreter in return for an upgrade to both his living conditions and his diet. Knowing that the English didn't understand German, he used his time with the Hessian soldiers encouraging them to desert. It's been estimated that he was successful in approximately 500 cases. After 18 months of imprisonment on the English prison ship, Solomon was paroled.

In 1778 he was again arrested and charged with being an American spy. The English confiscated his properties and sentenced him to be hanged. With the help of the Sons of Liberty and a bribed guard, he was able to escape. He made his way to Philadelphia, where his wife and child joined him. Once settled in Pennsylvania he reopened his brokerage business and rebuilt his fortune. By 1781 he was the American agent to the French consul and the paymaster for French forces in North America. It was during this period that Solomon provided financial support and loans with no interest to James Monroe, Thomas Jefferson, James Madison, and James Wilson. Most of these loans were never repaid.

Solomon's business continued to grow and eventually became the largest depositor in the Bank of North America run and owned by a signer of the Declaration of Independence, Robert Morris. The revolutionary government had appointed Morris to the post of Superintendent of Finance, and it was his responsibility to manage the economy. As the young nation faced one financial crisis after another, Morris turned to Solomon for help. Morris kept a detailed diary and the name Haym Solomon appears in it more than 75 times.

In 1781 General George Washington saw an opportunity to win the war that he had been fighting for more than half a decade. The British General Charles Cornwallis had suffered a series of defeats. He had retreated with his forces to Yorktown, Virginia where he waited for the British Navy to supply both supplies and reinforcements. The French fleet, however, defeated the English fleet and positioned themselves outside of the Chesapeake Bay effectively blocking any aid that could reach him by sea. With both the anticipated support and escape to the sea lost Cornwallis could only hope to escape by land. Instead, he decided to wait for help from British forces stationed in New York, and this presented Washington with the opportunity he saw and wished to use to his advantage.

Unfortunately for the American general, his army was underpaid, undersupplied, and underfed. Washington and his troops lacked the funds necessary to move south where they could trap the British force against the sea. The revolutionary treasury was empty, and Washington required funds to transport and feed his army. Washington appealed to Morris, who turned to Solomon for help. Within a day, the necessary funding was secured. Washington then led his forces south where they boxed in Cornwallis and forced his surrender. The siege of Yorktown proved to be the decisive battle in the successful American Revolution.

The end of the war did not mean that all was well financially in the young nation. By August of 1782, the United States Treasury was once again empty. The country had no credit left, and the economic situation was a threat to make meaningless the victories won on the American Revolution battlefields. Morris, as he detailed in his diary, once again turned to Haym Solomon for help. In the estimation of the Harvard historian Professor Albert Bushnell Hart, "Solomon's credit was better than that of the whole thirteen United States." Haym Solomon again did what was necessary for his country, and through his efforts, this crisis was averted.

After the war, Solomon did indeed turn his attention back to his business and his family. Though still a young man, his health deteriorated. Some believe that he had contracted tuberculosis during the time he was imprisoned by the British. He also suffered severe financial reverses, and when he died on January 6, 1785, he was bankrupt. Not a single loan drawn from his fortune and granted to the United States government and multiple revolutionary era figures was ever repaid. He was laid to rest in the Mikveh Israel Cemetery on Spruce Street in Philadelphia. His family could not afford a tombstone, and the grave was never marked. Thus the exact location is unknown. There are two plaque memorials at the site. There is also a sculpture, the Herald Square Monument located in Chicago, that shows George Washington flanked by Solomon and Morris and grasping hands with both men. The inscription at the base of the monument quotes the first President, "The Government of the United States, which gives to bigotry no sanction, to persecution no assistance, requires only that they who live under its protection should demean themselves as good citizens, in giving it all occasions their effectual support."

Solomon today remains one of the lesser-known founders who deserves far more recognition for his efforts on behalf of the new nation. It is not an exaggeration to state that without his assistance, the chances of the American Revolution ending successfully would have been greatly diminished. Like many of his contemporaries, current Americans remain in his debt.

Memorial to Haym Solomon in the cemetery where he is believed to be buried

George Taylor
(1716–1781)

Indentured Ironmaster

Buried at Easton Cemetery,
Easton, Pennsylvania.

—————•◦•—————

Declaration of Independence

George Taylor was a signer of the Declaration of Independence as a representative of Pennsylvania. He was born in Ireland in 1716 and was one of three signers of the Declaration born in Ireland. As a young man, he wanted to come to America but was too poor to pay his passage so he became an indentured servant to Samuel Savage who ran an iron foundry outside Philadelphia. Taylor went from being an indentured servant to a successful and respected businessman and citizen and signer of the historic Declaration of Independence.

————⧓•◦•⧓————

He arrived in 1736 and started as a laborer, but when Savage discovered that Taylor had a certain degree of education, he made him a clerk in his foundry. In 1742, Savage died and George married his widow, Ann, and took over the iron business. It prospered. He and Ann would have two children. He also had five children with his housekeeper Naomi Smith with whom he would carry on an affair for years.

Taylor moved to Easton in 1763 and became involved in public affairs. In 1767, the same year Ann died, he purchased land and built an impressive home in Catasauqua, about fifteen miles from Easton. This home, the George Taylor Mansion, still stands and is a National Historic

George Taylor

Landmark. He served in the provincial assembly from 1764 to 1769 and then was re-elected in 1775. There he helped draft the instructions to the delegates to the Continental Congress which called for voting against separation from Britain. As public sentiment changed, those instructions were rescinded in June 1776. As problems with Britain worsened Taylor spoke out in favor of independence. In July 1775, as colonial forces prepared for war, he was commissioned as a colonel in the Third Battalion of the Pennsylvania Militia. Also in 1775, he went to work at Durham Iron Works, which he leased and produced grapeshot, cannonballs, bar shot, and cannons for the Continental Army. This diminished his wealth as he received limited compensation from a strapped government.

In 1776, the Continental Congress voted for independence on July 2 and adopted the Declaration of Independence on July 4. Before the vote for independence, five of Pennsylvania's delegates, all loyalists, were forced to resign as the Congress had passed a proposal that stated, "for our mutual security and protection" no man could remain in Congress without signing. On July 20, Taylor was among the replacements appointed by the assembly. Others were Benjamin Rush, George Clymer, James Smith, and George Ross. One of his first duties was to affix his signature to the Declaration of Independence, which he did on August 2. The act of signing this momentous document was then considered an act of high treason against the British government and Crown. All the signers could be tried and executed and their property and estates confiscated

Of the 56 signers, he was one of only eight who were foreign-born, the only one to have been indentured, and the only ironmaster. He was elected to the First Supreme Executive Council of Pennsylvania in 1777 but soon became ill and retired from public life.

After George Taylor resigned from public office, he continued to support the patriots. From 1777 to 1780, Taylor worked at his iron mills, making cannonballs for the Continental Army. In 1780, Taylor became ill again and decided to return to his home in Easton. He spent the rest of his life there. He died on February 23, 1781, at the age of sixty-five. He sacrificed his estate for the Continental Army and did not live to see it's victory.

Taylor's body was originally buried at St. John's Lutheran Church in Easton. In 1854, a memorial was constructed in the Easton Cemetery for Taylor made of Italian marble. In 1870, his body was moved to the site of his memorial and was buried directly in front of it.

In Washington, D.C., near the Washington Monument, is a small park and lagoon dedicated to the memory of the signers of the Declaration of Independence, and one of the granite blocks there bears the name of "George Taylor."

The grave of George Taylor

Charles Thomson
(1729–1824)

Secretary of the Continental Congress

Buried at Laurel Hill Cemetery,
Philadelphia, Pennsylvania.

—————•—•—————

Secretary, Continental Congress

Although few people have heard of Charles Thomson, he was one of America's most significant and influential Founding Fathers. He served as the only Secretary of the Continental Congress for its entire fifteen years. He was a tremendous unifying factor. He kept the minutes of all sessions of Congress, including special minutes of all the secret meetings and deals. His journals and files became the archives of our nation. In all the factional disputes of the Revolutionary period, his judgment was respected. During the rumors and uncertainties of the Revolutionary War, Thomson helped the Continental Congress retain the faith and support of the people by insisting that full and honest reports be issued, under his signature, concerning all battles and engagements whether won or lost. His reputation was such that his reports were in high demand. When a congressional paper appeared containing his signature, the expression was frequently heard, "here comes the truth." Thomson's name was regarded as an emblem of truth.

—————◆•◆—————

Charles Thomson was born in 1729 in County Derry, Ireland to Scots-Irish parents. He was one of six children, and his mother died in

Charles Thomson

1739 during or shortly after the birth of his youngest sibling. Within a few months, his father John set out for Philadelphia with Charles and three of his older brothers. John became violently ill and died within sight of the shore. The ship was just off the capes of Delaware. The children were now left to the mercy of the sea captain, who embezzled the money which the father had brought with him and landed the boys ashore at New Castle, Delaware.

There Charles was separated from his brothers. He was placed in the care of a blacksmith who intended to make him an indentured servant. Through good fortune, he was admitted to the New London Academy in Chester County, Pennsylvania. While a student there, Thomson made the acquaintance of Benjamin Franklin and frequently sought his advice regarding the prospects of working in Philadelphia. Franklin, being President of the Board of Trustees of the new Academy of Philadelphia (the forerunner of the University of Pennsylvania), secured a position for Thomson at the school. He started as a tutor there on January 7, 1751.

He served as a tutor until 1755 and left to become head of the Latin department at Philadelphia's Friends Public School. In 1758 he married Ruth Mather, a member of a well-to-do Chester family. In 1760 he left teaching to enter into business. He and Ruth separated in 1769. In 1770 tragedy struck when their infant twins and Ruth died.

While at the Friends School, Thomson joined the Quakers in their opposition to the Penn family's Indian policy. He became the secretary for the Delaware Indians in 1756 at a great council held in Easton, Pennsylvania to resolve their differences with the settlers. The tribe adopted him as a son according to an ancient Indian custom. All during this time, he was allied with Ben Franklin, but they parted politically during the Stamp Act crisis in 1765. He then allied himself with John Dickinson. He worked diligently throughout the Revolutionary period to keep English goods out of Philadelphia. By 1773 he was writing fiery handbills against the importation of tea from the East India Company. During this decade Thomson was the colony's most powerful protest organizer. He became known as "the Sam Adams of Philadelphia." He also became a leader in Philadelphia's Sons of Liberty, a secret organization of landowners throughout the colonies formed to protect the rights of colonists and to fight taxation by the British government.

On September 1, 1774, Thomson married Hannah Harrison, the sister of Benjamin Harrison, who would become a signer of the Declaration of Independence. The following Monday, September 5, the First Continental Congress convened in Philadelphia and unanimously selected Thomson as Secretary.

He served over the next fifteen years as secretary to the first and second Continental Congresses and then to the Confederation Congress. Through those fifteen years, Congress saw many delegates come and go, but Thomson's dedication to recording the debates and decisions provided continuity. The Continental Congress was in some respects one of the most remarkable legislative bodies the world has ever seen. Thomson knew better than any other man the secret history of Congress and the motives which influenced its members. He beheld the development of

Obelisk honoring Charles Thomson

national consciousness, and he was present at the dawn of independence. Thomson's name appeared on the first published version of the Declaration of Independence as the only non-delegate signature. He signed in his capacity as Congressional Secretary.

Among his many accomplishments as Secretary, Thomson designed the Great Seal of the United States. The United States of America continues to use the Great Seal on all of its official documents. It can be easily found on the reverse side of the one-dollar bill.

Thomson's service was not without its critics, however. In 1780 delegate James Searle, a close friend of John Adams, began a cane fight on the floor of Congress, claiming that Thomson misquoted him in the minutes. Both men were slashed in the face. Thomson's recordings of events frequently led to arguments and fights on the floor of Congress.

Thomson was keenly aware of the slavery problem. He wrote to Jefferson in 1785: "It grieves me to the soul that there should be such grounds for your apprehensions respecting the irritation that will be produced in the southern states by what you have said of slavery. However, I would not have you discouraged. This is a cancer we must get rid of. It is a blot on our character that must be wiped out. If it cannot be done

The original gravestone for Charles Thomson

by religion, reason, and philosophy, confident I am that it will be done one day by blood."

Thomson's last official act as Secretary was to inform George Washington of his election. He traveled to Mt. Vernon on April 1789 to tell him officially that under the new constitution he had been elected the first President. By July, Thomson was retired, having turned over the Great Seal of the United States to Washington.

As Secretary of Congress, Thomson chose what to include in the official journals of the Continental Congress. He also prepared a work of over 1000 pages that covered the political history of the American Revolution. After leaving office, he chose to destroy this work, stating his desire to avoid "contradicting all the histories of the great events of the Revolution. Let the world admire the supposed wisdom and valor of our great men. Perhaps they may adopt the qualities that have been ascribed to them, and thus good may be done. I shall not undeceive future generations."

Charles Thomson died on August 16, 1824, at the age of 95. He had been residing in Bryn Mawr, Pennsylvania at Harriton House which still stands today and operates as a museum. He was initially buried there, but in 1838 his nephew moved his remains to Laurel Hill Cemetery in Philadelphia. A large handsome monument marks his grave.

Anthony Wayne
(1716–1778)

Mad Anthony

Buried at Garrison Hill, Erie, Pennsylvania, and
Old St. David Church Cemetery, Wayne, Pennsylvania.

―•―

Military

Anthony Wayne was one of the important military generals and statesmen who contributed extensively to the American Revolution. Had he
not died suddenly at the age of 51, he might have given John Adams or
Thomas Jefferson a real challenge for the presidency in 1796 and 1800.

―•―

Wayne was born on New Year's Day, 1745, in Chester County,
Pennsylvania, and attended a private school in Philadelphia operated by
his uncle. He eventually became an excellent surveyor and in 1765 was
sent to Nova Scotia as a financial agent and surveyor in the service of
a real estate company on the recommendation of Benjamin Franklin.
He returned to the United States in 1767, married, and continued in
his profession as well as serving in several local offices. In 1774, his father Isaac died and Anthony inherited his prosperous tannery business.
Also that year, he was chosen as one of the provincial representatives to
consider the relations between the colonies and Great Britain and was a
member of the Pennsylvania convention that was held in Philadelphia to
discuss this matter.

Wayne served in the Pennsylvania legislature in 1775. He was fond
of military affairs. He began studying works on the art of war, and at the

Anthony Wayne

onset of the Revolutionary War raised a militia. In 1776, Wayne became colonel of the 4th Pennsylvania Regiment. He and his regiment were part of the Continental Army's failed invasion of Canada. He attacked the British at the Battle of Three Rivers and although wounded and defeated, withdrew his troops creditably and then was ordered to assume command at Fort Ticonderoga.

In February 1777, Wayne was commissioned a brigadier general. Prior to the war, Wayne had no military experience and other more experienced officers resented his quick advancement. He became known for his bravado and ill-advised attacks. He earned the nickname "Mad" Anthony Wayne because of his impulsive actions on the battlefield. Wayne was known for his fiery temper and would rather attack the enemy than avoid them.

Later in 1777, he assisted George Washington in the failed defense of the nation's capital, Philadelphia. He commanded troops at Brandywine,

Germantown, and Paoli. The British surprise attack at Paoli on September 20, 1777, was a dark moment for Wayne. He lost a lot of men, and some of his officers thought he handled it poorly. Wayne's temper took hold, and he demanded first an official inquiry and then a full court-martial. The court-martial unanimously exonerated Wayne and acquitted him "with the highest honor." Washington heartily approved.

Washington relied heavily on Wayne throughout the war. Before making strategic decisions, it was Washington's habit to have his top general's write out their suggestions. He could always count on Wayne to propose aggressive and well-thought-out plans.

During the winter of 1777-78, Wayne did much to supply the American camp at Valley Forge. In March, he made a successful raid into British lines, capturing horses, cattle, and other needed supplies. In June of 1778, he led the American attack at the Battle of Monmouth. It was the first time Americans held their own in toe-to-toe battle with the British troops.

The highlight of Wayne's Revolutionary War service was his victory at Stony Point, New York on July 16, 1779. Washington had asked Wayne to form and command an elite "American Light Corps" (the equivalent of today's Special Forces). Wayne led his troops in a carefully planned, nighttime, surprise attack against a heavily fortified stronghold on top of a steep Hudson River palisade. The assault was successful and Wayne's troops captured the fort and its occupants. Wayne himself received a severe scalp wound. Before dawn, Wayne sent Washington a message that read: "The fort and garrison with Colonel Johnston are ours. Our officers and men behaved like men who are determined to be free."

The assault at Stony Point was widely recognized as one of the most brilliant maneuvers of the war. Congress unanimously passed resolutions praising Wayne and awarded him a gold medal commemorative. The Continental Army had experienced few successes. This victory, led personally by General Wayne, substantially improved the soldiers' morale.

In 1780, Wayne helped put down a mutiny of 1,300 Pennsylvania men who had not received payment from the government. He did so by serving as the men's advocate before the Confederation Congress, where he arranged an agreement to the advantage of the government and the satisfaction of the men.

In the summer of 1781, just before the Battle of Yorktown, Wayne saved a Continental Army force led by the Marquis de Lafayette from a trap set by the commander of the British Army, Lieutenant General Lord Cornwallis, near Williamsburg, Virginia. Wayne's small contingent of 800 Pennsylvanians was the vanguard of the continental forces. They were crossing over a swamp by a narrow causeway when they were ambushed by over 4,000 British. Instead of retreating, Wayne charged. The unexpected maneuver so surprised the enemy that they fell back confused allowing the rest of Lafayette's command to avoid the trap.

After the British surrender at Yorktown on October 19, 1781, Wayne went further south and severed the British alliance with Native American tribes in Georgia. He negotiated peace treaties with both the Creek and Cherokee, for which Georgia rewarded him with the gift of a large rice plantation. In October 1783 he was promoted to major general and retired from the Continental Army.

Wayne returned to Pennsylvania and resumed his civilian life. In 1784, he was elected to the general assembly from Chester County and served in the convention that ratified the Constitution of the United States. He then moved to Georgia and was elected to the Second United States Congress in 1791. He lost that seat during a debate over his residency qualifications and declined to run for reelection.

President Washington showed his high regard for Wayne once again in 1792 when he recalled him from civilian life and appointed Wayne as the commanding general of the newly-formed "Legion of the United States." At the end of the Revolutionary War, Great Britain agreed that the Mississippi River would be the western boundary of the United States and that the Great Lakes would be the northern border. Presumably, this meant British troops would withdraw from these areas into Canada. In fact, they did not. They encouraged and supplied a Western Indian Confederacy led by Blue Jacket of the Shawnees and Little Turtle of the Miamis. The Indians had achieved major victories over U.S. forces in 1790 under command of General Josiah Harmar and in 1791 under command of General Arthur St. Clair. More than 700 Americans died in the fighting.

Wayne recruited troops from the Pittsburgh area and established a basic training facility at Legionville to prepare the men of the "Legion of the United States" for battle. Located in Beaver County, Legionville was the first facility ever established to provide basic training for U.S. Army recruits.

In August 1794, Wayne mounted an assault on the Indian confederacy at the Battle of Fallen Timbers near Toledo, Ohio. It was a decisive victory for the U.S. forces and ended for all time the power of the British on American soil.

Wayne then negotiated the Treaty of Greenville between the Indian tribes and the United States. The treaty was signed in August 1795 and gave most of what is now Ohio to the United States. He returned home to a hero's welcome in the Philadelphia area.

In June 1796, Wayne was back in the frontier overseeing the surrender of British forts to the U.S. In a visit to Fort Presque Isle in Erie, Pennsylvania, he suffered a serious gout attack. There were no physicians at the fort and calls went out to Pittsburgh and the Army hospitals. Unfortunately, help arrived too late, and Anthony Wayne died on December 15, 1796.

A year earlier at Fort Presque Isle, to assist in defending against attacks from Native Americans, 200 Federal troops from Wayne's army under the direction of Captain John Grubb built a blockhouse on a bluff there known as Garrison Hill. Wayne had requested that upon his death he be buried there. When he died, his body was placed in a plain oak coffin, his initials and date of death were driven into the wood using round-headed brass tacks, and his request was honored. He was buried at the foot of the blockhouse's flagstaff on Garrison Hill.

Twelve years later, Wayne's son, Isaac, rode to Erie in a small, two-wheeled carriage called a sulky. He came (at the urging of his sister Peggy) to bring his father's remains back to be buried in the family plot at Old St. David Church about 400 miles away outside of Philadelphia. Young Wayne enlisted the help of Dr. J. G. Wallace, who had been with Mad Anthony at the Battle of Fallen Timbers and at his side when he died.

When Wallace opened Wayne's coffin, he found little decay except in the lower portion of one leg. This caused a dilemma, as Isaac did not have enough space to transport the entire body. He expected to put bones in boxes on his sulky. Dr. Wallace used a custom common to

American Indians to solve the dilemma. He dismembered the body and boiled it in a large iron kettle until the flesh dropped off. He cleaned the bones and packed them into Isaac's boxes. The task was so distasteful that Dr. Wallace threw the remaining tissue and his instruments into the coffin and closed the grave. Isaac Wayne made the long journey across Pennsylvania with his father's bones in the back of his sulky. The bones were interred at Old St. David Church Cemetery with funeral rites celebrated on July 4, 1809. A huge crowd attended.

General Anthony Wayne is well-memorialized. He has a long list of cities, towns, and municipalities named after him, including 15 states that have a Wayne County. In Pennsylvania, there is a Wayne County as well as a Waynesboro and a Waynesburg. He has schools, bridges, a university (Wayne State University in Detroit), a brewing company (Mad Anthony Brewing Co. in Fort Wayne, Indiana), an ale (Mad Anthony Ale, a product of Erie Brewing Co.), a hotel (General Wayne Inn in Merion, PA), parks, hospitals, and even a barbershop named in his honor.

The original grave of Anthony Wayne near Erie

The final resting place of the bones of Anthony Wayne at Old
Saint David Church Cemetery in Wayne, Pennsylvania

There is a large statue in Fort Wayne, Indiana, as well as a gilded bronze
equestrian statue at the Philadelphia Museum of Art and one at Valley
Forge. In 1929, the U.S. Post Office issued a stamp honoring Wayne and
commemorating the 150th anniversary of the Battle of Fallen Timbers.

Anthony Wayne's strange interment has given rise to a popular ghost
story. It was a long, tough trip from Erie to Wayne over 380 miles of
unpaved roads of what is now Route 322. The story goes that Isaac had
many problems along the way and that the trunk kept falling off and
breaking open, losing bones along the way. Some claim that on each New
Year's Day (Wayne's birthday), his ghost rises from his grave in Wayne
and rides across the state searching for his missing bones. The kettle used
to boil Wayne's body and the dissection instruments used by Dr. Wallace
are on display at the Erie County History Center on State Street in Erie.

Thomas Willing
(1731–1821)

Banker and Financier

Buried at Christ Church Burial Ground,
Philadelphia, Pennsylvania.

Financier

Thomas Willing was the son of Philadelphia mayor Charles Willing (1710-1754) and his wife, Anne Shippen, heir to one of the prominent families in Pennsylvania and the granddaughter of Edward Shippen, Philadelphia's second mayor. Willing was a delegate to the Continental Congress but refused to sign the Declaration of Independence. Instead, he focused on organizing the finances of the young republic and was president of the Bank of North American and the first president of the Bank of the United States.

Willing was born December 19, 1731, in Philadelphia, Pennsylvania. He first attended preparatory school at Bath, England, followed by law studies at the Inner Temple in London and business studies at Watts Academy.

His education completed, in 1749 Willing returned to Philadelphia where he worked in his father's mercantile business selling dry goods on short-term credit. Having developed a strong conservative business sense, the younger Willing was elevated to a partner in 1751. Upon his father's unexpected death in 1754, the 23-year-old became solely responsible

Thomas Willing

for the family's financial interests, taking care of his mother and nine younger siblings. He also managed the estates, wills, and trusts of other wealthy families.

Willing continued to expand his business interests in the 1750s, adding wet goods such as alcohol to the mix as well as entering the slave trade. He also invested in real estate, traded in mortgages, and underwrote marine insurance at cheaper rates than the London firms. In 1757, Willing joined forces with Robert Morris to establish the firm Willing, Morris, and Company, which was one of the most successful businesses in the colonies, transporting, importing, and exporting goods between Maryland, Virginia, and Europe. Morris later became the financier of the American Revolution and was at one point considered by some to be second to only George Washington in influence. Unlike Morris, however, Willing was less of a risk-taker and did not suffer the economic collapse later experienced by his partner.

Willing was active in city politics before the Revolution, holding several offices in the 1750s and 1760s, including Common Councilman, Judge of the Orphan's Court, and Mayor of Philadelphia in 1763. On behalf of Pennsylvania, he attended the Albany Congress, oversaw trade with the Indians, and organized the survey of the boundary with Maryland. He was also a member of the Pennsylvania Assembly from 1764 to 1767. He resigned when appointed by the Penns to become a justice on the Pennsylvania Supreme Court where he served for ten years, along with Thomas Lawrence, as the last under colonial rule. For 31 years, from 1760 until 1791, Willing was a trustee of the College of Philadelphia, now the University of Pennsylvania, serving as treasurer of the board of trustees for a time.

On a personal note, in 1763, Willing married Anne McCall (1745-1781), daughter of Samuel McCall, one of the founders of the University of Philadelphia, and Anne Searle, the daughter of Captain John Searle. The couple produced thirteen children.

With the passage of the Stamp Act in 1765, Willing found his profits significantly impacted. He was a leader of the protest and was the first signer of the Nonimportation Resolution, creating an embargo of British goods pending the repeal of the Act.

With tensions rising between the colonies and the mother country, Willing became active in the Revolutionary cause speaking publicly about unfair taxation. In 1774, he became a member of the Committee of Correspondence. He was also president of the first Provincial Congress of Pennsylvania, which sent petitions to Britain asking for the restoration of constitutional liberties to the colonies. The following year, he was a member of the Committee of Safety. He was appointed to the Continental Congress for 1775 and 1776, but, given his respect for the Penn family and his belief the colonies were not prepared for war, voted against the Declaration of Independence. This effectively ended his political career. He was not re-elected to the Congress.

Still a patriot, Willing continued to work for the cause, obtaining supplies and funding. However, he was criticized for selling these goods and loaning money rather than donating to the army. He also remained in Philadelphia during the British occupation but refused to swear an oath of loyalty to the king. He continued to work secretly against British interests.

In 1778, Thomas's brother James Willing led a series of raids known as the Willing Expedition to take British holdings in British West Florida, along the Mississippi River, now Natchez, Mississippi. James, also a member of the Continental Congress, had traveled to Natchez to convince the residents to join the Revolutionary cause and secure the Mississippi River for the Americans as the fourteenth state. While well-received, James's proposal was rejected by the mostly loyalist residents. So, he returned to Philadelphia and was commissioned a captain. He then led the expedition against Natchez, funded mainly by Robert Morris, traveling with a

The grave of Thomas Willing

crew of 29 from Fort Pitt in the gunboat USS *Rattletrap*, down the Ohio and Mississippi Rivers to raid the settlements. After numerous raids, Willing's Expedition ran out of steam and sought refuge in New Orleans. On his return to Philadelphia, James was captured by the British. He was later exchanged for a British officer.

Meanwhile, in Philadelphia, Robert Morris and his partner Thomas Willing convinced the Congress to form a bank that could lend money to the colonies and stabilize the currency. In 1781, the Bank of North America was founded, and Willing was its president. Later, following the adoption of the U.S. Constitution, wholeheartedly supported by Willing, Alexander Hamilton implemented a new financial system. Thomas Willing led his Bank of the United States as president until he suffered a stroke in 1807. The Bank of the United States under Willing's leadership helped stabilize the U.S. economy through the War of 1812.

His ability to speak limited by the effects of the stroke, Willing retired from public life and his business activities. He lived in Philadelphia until his death on January 19, 1821, a few weeks after his eighty-ninth birthday. Willing was buried in the Christ Church graveyard.

James Wilson
(1742–1798)

A Legal Theorist

Buried at Christ Episcopal Churchyard,
Philadelphia, Pennsylvania.

—•◦•—

**Declaration of Independence • U.S. Constitution
Supreme Court Justice**

This founder was born in Scotland. He was educated at several Scottish universities including Edinburgh and Saint Andrews. He came to America in search of the opportunities offered by the new world. He would make his way in the legal profession becoming well known as a brilliant jurist. He would join in the cause of American independence and sign both the Declaration of Independence and the United States Constitution. He was appointed to the United States Supreme Court by President Washington. His name was James Wilson.

—◦◦◦—

Wilson was born on September 14, 1742, in Carskerdo, Scotland. He was a Scottish farmboy who trained for the Presbyterian ministry at prestigious universities though he never graduated with a degree. In 1765 Wilson arrived in America and settled in Philadelphia determined to make his fortune. Initially, he became a teacher at the College of Philadelphia but soon devoted himself to the study of law under John Dickinson. After being admitted to the bar, he moved to Carlisle, Pennsylvania where he set up a successful law practice. Within a decade of his arrival

James Wilson

in the country, Wilson was recognized as one of the outstanding colonial leaders in the struggle against Great Britain.

In 1771, Wilson married Rachel Bird. The couple produced six children. Rachel passed away in 1786, and Wilson married Hannah Gray in 1793. They had one son named Henry who died at the age of three.

Wilson's treatise titled *Considerations on the Nature and Extent of the Legislative Authority of the British Parliament* was published in 1774. Some viewed it as the most learned and far-reaching statement of the colonial case against the mother country. Wilson took the position that Parliament lacked the authority to pass laws relative to the American colonies because the colonies were not represented in that body.

By the year 1776, Wilson was serving as a member of the Continental Congress representing Pennsylvania. As noted by the historian Pauline Maier, Wilson, who she described as having "advanced views on the constitutional structure of the empire," was also "one of Congress's great foot-draggers" on the question of American independence. On January

9, 1776, Wilson proposed that Congress vote to disavow any desire for independence. Those who opposed the proposal were able to postpone the question. On February 13, Wilson put forth an address to the people that was described by Richard Smith as "very long, badly written and full against Independency." According to Smith, the majority rejected Wilson's arguments, and he abandoned his proposal and never raised the subject again. In mid-May, Wilson noted that Pennsylvania had bound its delegates from approving anything that did not further improve relations between the colonies and England. It is evident that by July, things in Pennsylvania had changed and Wilson joined Benjamin Franklin and John Morton voting in favor of independence. Two members of the Pennsylvania delegation voted no, and two other representatives abstained so the three aye votes resulted in a narrow majority. Wilson proudly signed the Declaration of Independence.

Wilson was one of the most active members of the Continental Congress. He served on the Committee of Spies along with John Adams, Thomas Jefferson, John Rutledge, and Robert Livingston. He was also active relative to relations with American Indian tribes. He was described as the most influential delegate in laying down the general outline that governed the affairs of Congress with the border tribes. In1954 the American historian Page Smith wrote that as a member of Congress Wilson "performed greater services than any other member of that distinguished group of Continental statesmen."

In 1779 Wilson demonstrated his skills as an attorney after the British had abandoned the city of Philadelphia. He successfully defended 23 Tories, those who had remained loyal to the crown, from property seizure and exile by the government of Pennsylvania. A mob motivated by liquor and the speeches of Joseph Reed, President of Pennsylvania's Supreme Executive Council, formed and armed with two cannon marched to the sound of drums to Wilson's home on Third and Walnut Streets. When they reached Wilson's house, they began the assault on what would come to be known as Fort Wilson. Shots were fired from both sides. Only the arrival of the First City Troop saved the lives of Wilson and those who had taken refuge inside. On the street, one boy and one man lay dead, and many in the mob were arrested. Inside the Fort Wilson, one man,

Captain Campbell, was killed and two others were wounded. The arrested members of the mob were subsequently pardoned and released by order of Reed.

By the time the Constitutional Convention convened in 1787, Wilson was one of the most prominent and respected lawyers in America. He once again represented Pennsylvania at that gathering, and his performance did not disappoint. In his book *1787 The Grand Convention,* which is still hailed as among the best accounts of the meeting that produced the Constitution, Clinton Rossiter rates Wilson's performance second only to that of James Madison. Rossiter terms it an honorable second noting that Wilson "debated, drafted, bargained, and voted with unremitting zeal. He did most to give strength to the executive, and to lay the foundations of the new government broad and deep upon the sovereign people of the United States." Similar sentiments can be found in *The Founders Coup: The Making of the United States Constitution* authored by Michael J. Klarman. In this volume, Wilson is said to be one of the three or four most important delegates. In Klarman's view, Wilson was "among the foremost in legal and political knowledge." Klarman points out that Wilson had made the study of government and the political institutions of the world a life long study. The wisdom he shared at the convention cemented his place in history. When the Constitution was adopted, Wilson was once again a proud signer of that historic document.

Wilson was an active participant in the fight for ratification of the Constitution. He is recognized as the leading voice of those who favored ratification in the state of Pennsylvania. As a delegate to the state convention, he answered virtually every argument raised against the Constitution with a clarity and eloquence that was to be expected from one of the great legal minds of his time. The divisions in Pennsylvania relative to ratification were put on display in Carlisle where a mob burned Wilson in effigy after receiving word that the state convention had voted in favor of ratification.

President Washington nominated Wilson to be a Justice on the United States Supreme Court on September 24, 1789. He was confirmed by the Senate and served on the court until 1798. Not unlike some of his fellow founders, Wilson's final days were marked by financial failures.

He found himself deep in debt as a result of investing in land that became liabilities as a result of the Panic of 1796. He was imprisoned in a New Jersey debtors prison for a short time but was released after his son satisfied the obligation. He then fled to North Carolina to elude other creditors. He was visiting a friend in North Carolina when he suffered a stroke and died at the age of 55. He was initially laid to rest in North Carolina, but in 1906 his remains were reinterred in the Christ Episcopal Churchyard in Philadelphia. Dr. Benjamin Rush, a fellow delegate at the Constitutional Convention, described Wilson's mind as "one blaze of light." That light still shines through the United States Constitution and remains bright in the two centuries that have passed since its ratification.

The grave of James Wilson

Revolutionary War Sites in Pennsylvania

———•—•———

Pennsylvania was dubbed the Keystone State for a reason. During the formative years of the nation, it was in the middle of the thirteen colonies in their north/south orientation. Philadelphia was the largest city in the British Empire in the New World and served as the hub for a greater share of activity in the colonial period. During the American Revolution, Philadelphia and its environs were the settings for many significant events of our nation's founding.

In the heart of the old city, the most important sites are those related to the founding of the government of the United States. Independence National Historical Park includes Independence Hall, where the Declaration of Independence and the Constitution were debated and adopted. Across the street is the Liberty Bell Center which houses the famous Liberty Bell. Also in the park are the First Bank of the United States, the Second Bank of the United States, Franklin Court, Benjamin Franklin Museum, and Carpenter's Hall, the site of the First Continental Congress.

City Tavern is nearby and is a great place to stop for a drink or a meal. The tavern is restored to the period and is on the site where the original tavern stood. Many of the founders frequented it during their time in Congress or while passing through town.

In the Independence Mall area, on the boundaries of the park, the National Constitution Center is a facility that honors the U.S. Constitution. However, the original document is stored at the National Archives in Washington, D.C.

The Delaware River at Washington's Crossing looking toward New Jersey.

Also in or near Independence Mall is the recently built Museum of the American Revolution, which does a fantastic job of interpreting the narrative and artifacts of the Revolution. The Graff House or Declaration House is a few blocks from the park and is the site where Thomas Jefferson and the other committee members met to work on the Declaration of Independence.

Also in the city, at the Franklin Institute, is the Benjamin Franklin National Memorial including a large statue of Franklin in the rotunda. The Betsy Ross House honors the first flag of the United States. Christ Church is the final resting place of Benjamin Franklin and many other founders. The Thaddeus Kosciuszko National Memorial honors the Polish general at his restored home. The Rosenbach Museum stores many rare books and manuscripts related to the Revolution.

To get a sense of colonial period, Elfreth's Alley is a nearby neighborhood that includes rows of historic homes that are nicely maintained. The street retains the cobbles from long ago.

At Washington Square is located the Tomb of the Unknown Revolutionary War Soldier which honors the thousands who gave their lives for the cause. Many are buried in a mass grave under that square.

In the surrounding suburbs can be found the following sites:

- Graeme Park in Horsham includes the historic Keith House from the colonial period.
- Harriton House in Bryn Mawr was the home of Charles Thomson, secretary of the Continental Congress.
- Hope Lodge is the home of Samuel Morris built in the colonial period. It is near Fort Washington.
- Pennypacker Mills near Schwenksville served as the headquarters for George Washington prior the Battle of Germantown. It then served as a field hospital during and after the battle.
- Peter Wentz Farmstead near Lansdale also served as a headquarters for George Washington before and after the Battle of Germantown.
- Waynesborough, also known as the General Anthony Wayne House, is near Paoli.
- The Speaker's House located in Trappe is the former home of Frederick Muhlenberg, the first Speaker of the House of Representatives.

Monument at Washington's Crossing

For those interested in military history, Fort Mifflin, built in 1771, was attacked and taken by the British during their invasion of Philadelphia. The Brandywine Battlefield is a national historic site. The Paoli battlefield is managed by a private nonprofit organization. A visit to the Germantown battlefield must include a visit to Cliveden, a preserved colonial home at the center of the action. Unfortunately, all these are sites where colonial forces lost to the British. For a more uplifting experience, Washington Crossing State Park includes a museum and grounds from which George Washington launched the successful battles at Princeton and Trenton across the Delaware River.

Lastly, there are two encampment sites near Philadelphia. At Fort Washington State Park in the Whitemarsh area, you can walk where Washington's troops camped after the defeat at Germantown before moving to Valley Forge.

At Valley Forge National Historical Park, the grounds where the Continental Army suffered terribly during the brutal winter of 1777/1778 are preserved. This expansive park includes many restored buildings and memorials.

Leaving the Philadelphia area to the north, the Liberty Bell Museum in Allentown is in the Zion's United Church of Christ which hid the Liberty Bell during the Revolution.

Heading west from Philadelphia to Pottstown, Pottsgrove Manor is a colonial-era home built by John Potts.

Further west, near Birdsboro, which is between Pottstown and Reading, Hopewell Furnace National Historic Site is a colonial-era iron-makers village that includes numerous homes from the period.

Another iron furnace on the way to Lancaster can be found at Cornwall. This state historic site is open for tours.

The Rock Ford Plantation in Lancaster is the former home of Major General Edward Hand.

When the Continental Congress fled Philadelphia, they briefly stopped in Lancaster and used its courthouse as a meeting place for one day. That building no longer exists. However, after Congress crossed the Susquehanna River, they found safety in York, Pennsylvania. There, the Articles of Confederation were debated and adopted by the Second

Detail on the memorial at Washington's Crossing

Statue of Baron von Steuben at Valley Forge

Cabins at Valley Forge National Historical Park

Statue of George Washington at Valley Forge

Continental Congress which called York home for nearly nine months between September 1777 and June 1778. The York County Heritage Trust Colonial Complex includes the old courthouse in which the Congress met and the Golden Plough Tavern. Nearby is the General Horatio Gates House.

In western Pennsylvania, at Pittsburgh, The Fort Pitt Museum at Point State Park includes exhibits about the colonial period and the Revolution.

There are many more sites not mentioned found throughout the state. Only historical markers along the road represent many. Others are private homes or open by appointment. The Keystone State is rich with history from the Revolution and the entire history of our nation.

Lastly, as the second most populous state during the Revolution (Virginia was the most populated), Pennsylvania's historic cemeteries are often the last resting places of numerous patriots. Many of these old churchyards have dozens of Revolutionary War soldiers buried in them. Each one played an essential role in our nation's founding and should not be forgotten.

Sources

Books, Magazines, Journals, Files:

Appleby, Joyce. *Inheriting the Revolution: The First Generation of Americans*. Cambridge, Massachusetts: Harvard University Press, 2000.

Atkinson, Rick. *The British Are Coming: The War for America, Lexington to Princeton, 1775-1777*. New York: Henry Holt & Co. 2019.

Bordewich, Fergus M. *The First Congress: How James Madison, George Washington, and a Group of Extraordinary Men Invented the Government*. New York: Simon and Schuster Paperbacks, 2016.

Boudreau, George W. *Independence: A Guide to Historic Philadelphia*. Yardley, Pennsylvania: Westholme Publishing, LLC. 2012.

Bowen, Catherine Drinker. *Miracle at Philadelphia: The Story of the Constitutional Convention May to September 1787*. Boston, Massachusetts: Little, Brown & Company, 1966.

Breen, T.H, *George Washington's Journey: The President Forges a New Nation*. New York: Simon & Schuster. 2016.

Brookhiser, Richard. *Gentleman Revolutionary: Gouverneur Morris The Rake Who Wrote the Constitution*. New York: Free Press, 2003.

———. *John Marshall: The Man Who Made the Supreme Court*. New York: Basic Books. 2018.

Chadwick, Bruce. *I Am Murdered: George Wythe, Thomas Jefferson, and the Killing That Shocked a New Nation*. Hoboken, New Jersey: John Wiley & Sons, 2009.

Chambers, II, John Whiteclay. *The Oxford Companion to American Military History*. Oxford: Oxford University Press, 1999.

Commager, Henry Steele & Richard B. Morris. *The Spirit of 'Seventy-Six: The Story of the American Revolution as Told by Participants*. New York: Harper & Rowe, 1967.

Cole, Ryan. *Light-Horse Harry Lee: The Rise and Fall of a Revolutionary Hero*. Washington, D.C.: Regnery History. 2019.

Conlin, Joseph R. *The Morrow Book of Quotations in American History*. New York: William Morrow and Company, Inc., 1984.

Daniels, Jonathan. *Ordeal of Ambition*. Garden City, New York: Doubleday & Company, Inc., 1970.

Dann, John C. *The Revolution Remembered: Eyewitness Accounts of the War for Independence*. Chicago: University of Chicago Press, 1980.

DeRose, Chris. *Founding Rivals: Madison vs. Monroe: The Bill of Rights and the Election that Saved a Nation*. New York: MJF Books, 2011.

Drury, Bob & Tom Clavin. *Valley Forge*. New York: Simon & Schuster. 2018.

Ellis, Joseph J. *Revolutionary Summer: The Birth of American Independence*. New York: Alfred A. Knopf, 2013.

———. *The Quartet: Orchestrating the Second American Revolution, 1783-1789*. New York: Alfred A. Knopf, 2015.

————. *His Excellency: George Washington.* New York: Alfred A. Knopf, 2004.

Fleming, Thomas. *Duel: Alexander Hamilton, Aaron Burr and the Future of America.* New York: Basic Books, 1999.

Flexner, James Thomas. *George Washington in the American Revolution, 1775-1783.* Boston: Little, Brown & Company, 1967.

Flower, Lenore Embick. "Visit of President George Washington to Carlisle, 1794." Carlisle, Pennsylvania: The Hamilton Library and Cumberland County Historical Society, 1932.

Graeff, Arthur D. *Conrad Weiser: Pennsylvania Peacemaker.* Mechanicsburg, Pennsylvania. Distelfink Press. 2019.

Griffith, IV, William R. *The Battle of Lake George: England's First Triumph in the French and Indian War.* Charleston, South Carolina: The History Press, 2016.

Grossman, Mark. *Encyclopedia of the Continental Congress.* Armenia, New York: Grey House Publishing, 2015.

Hamilton, Edward P. *Fort Ticonderoga: Key to a Continent.* Boston: Little, Brown & Company, 1964.

Hocker, Edward H. *The Fighting Parson of the American Revolution.* Philadelphia: Edward H. Hocker. 1936.

Isenberg, Nancy. *Fallen Founder: The Life of Aaron Burr.* New York: Penguin Group, 2007.

Kennedy, Roger G. *Burr, Hamilton, and Jefferson: A Study in Character.* New York: Oxford University Press, 1999.

Kiernan, Denise & Joseph D'Agnese. *Signing Their Lives Away: The Fame and Misfortune of the Men Who Signed the Declaration of Independence.* Philadelphia: Quirk Books, 2008.

————. *Signing Their Rights Away: The Fame and Misfortune of the Men Who Signed the United States Constitution.* Philadelphia: Quirk Books, 2011.

Klarman, Michael J. *The Framers' Coup: The Making of the United States Constitution.* New York: Oxford University Press, 2016.

Langguth, A. J. *Patriots.* New York: Simon and Schuster, 1988.

Larson, Edward J. *A Magnificent Catastrophe.* New York: Free Press, 2007.

Lee, Mike. *Written Out of History: The Forgotten Founders Who Fought Big Government.* New York: Penguin Books, 2017.

Lewis, James E., Jr., *The Burr Conspiracy: Uncovering the Story Of an Early American Crisis,* Princeton: Princeton University Press, 2017.

Lomask, Milton. *Aaron Burr: The Years from Princeton to Vice President, 1756-1805.* New York: Farrar Straus Giroux, 1979.

Lossing, Benson J. *Pictorial Field Book of the Revolution.* New York: Harper Brothers. 1851.

Maier, Pauline. *American Scripture: Making the Declaration of Independence.* New York: Alfred A. Knopf, Inc., 1997.

McCullough, David. *John Adams.* New York: Simon & Schuster, 2002.

Meltzer, Brad & Josh Mensch. *The First Conspiracy: The Secret Plot to Kill George Washington.* New York: Flat Iron Books. 2018.

Middlekauff, Robert. *The Glorious Cause: The American Revolution, 1763-1789.* Oxford: Oxford University Press, 2005.

Miller, Jr., Arthur P. & Marjorie L. Miller. *Pennsylvania Battlefields and Military Landmarks.* Mechanicsburg, Pennsylvania: Stackpole Books, 2000.

Millett, Allan R. & Peter Maslowski. *For the Common Defense: A Military History of the United States of America.* New York: The Free Press, 1984.

Minardi, Lisa. *Pastors and Patriots: The Muhlenberg Family of Pennsylvania.* Kutztown, Pennsylvania: The Pennsylvania German Society. 2011

Moore, Charles. *The Family Life of George Washington.* New York: Houghton Mifflin, 1926.

Nagel, Paul C.. *The Lees of Virginia: Seven Generations of an American Family.* Oxford: Oxford University Press, 1990.

O'Connell, Robert L. *Revolutionary: George Washington at War.* New York: Random House. 2019.

Racove, Jack N. *Revolutionaries: A New History of the Invention of America.* New York: Houghton Mifflin Harcourt, 2011.

Raphael, Ray. *Founding Myths: Stories That Hide Our Patriotic Past.* New York: MJF Books, 2004.

Rossiter, Clinton. *1787 The Grand Convention.* New York: The Macmillan Company, 1966.

Seymour, Joseph. *The Pennsylvania Associators, 1747-1777.* Yardley, Pennsylvania: Westholme Publishing, LLC. 2012.

Schweikart, Larry & Michael Allen. *A Patriot's History of the United States from Columbus's Great Discovery to the War on Terror.* New York: Penguin, 2004.

Sedgwick, John. *War of Two: Alexander Hamilton, Aaron Burr and the Duel That Stunned The Nation.* New York: Berkley Books, 2015.

Sharp, Arthur G. *Not Your Father's Founders.* Avon, Massachusetts: Adams Media, 2012.

Taafee, Stephen R. *The Philadelphia Campaign, 1777-1778.* Lawrence, Kansas: University of Kansas Press, 2003.

Tinkcom, Harry Marlin, *The Republicans and the Federalists in Pennsylvania, 1790-1801.* Harrisburg, Pennsylvania: Pennsylvania Historical and Museum Commission. 1950.

Wagner, William Muhlenberg, Jr. *The Muhlenberg Family: Their Significance in Colonial America.* Morgantown, Pennsylvania: Masthof Press. 2006.

Wallace, Paul A.W. *The Muhlenbergs of Pennsylvania.* Philadelphia: University of Pennsylvania Press, 1950

Ward, Matthew C. *Breaking the Backcountry: The Seven Years' War in Virginia and Pennsylvania, 1754-1765.* Pittsburgh, Pennsylvania: University of Pittsburgh Press, 2003.

Weisberger, Bernard A. *America Afire: Jefferson, Adams, and the Revolutionary Election of 1800.* New York: HarperCollins, 2000.

Williams, Roger M. "Who's Got Button's Bones?" *American Heritage.* Volume 17, Issue 2 (February 1966).

SOURCES

Wood, Gordon S. *The Radicalism of the American Revolution.* New York: Vintage Books, 1993.

———. *Empire of Liberty: A History of the Early Republic, 1789-1815.* New York: Penguin Books, 2004.

———. *Revolutionary Characters: What Made the Founders Different.* New York: Penguin Books, 2006.

———. *The Americanization of Benjamin Franklin.* Oxford: Oxford University Press, 2009.

Wright, Benjamin F. *The Federalist: The Famous Papers on the Principles of American Government: Alexander Hamilton, James Madison, John Jay.* New York: Metro Books, 2002.

Young, Alfred F. *Masquerade: The Life and Times of Deborah Sampson, Continental Soldier.* New York: Alfred A. Knopf, 2004.

———. *The Shoemaker and the Tea Party: Memory and the American Revolution.* Boston: Beacon Press, 1999.

Zambone, Albert Louis. *Daniel Morgan: A Revolutionary Life.* Yardley, Pennsylvania: Westholme Publishing, LLC. 2019.

Zobel, Hiller B. *The Boston Massacre.* New York: W. W. Norton & Company, 1970.

Video Resources:

Guelzo, Allen C. *The Great Courses: America's Founding Fathers (Course N. 8525).* Chantilly, Virginia: The Teaching Company, 2017.

Online Resources:

Archives.gov – for information on the Constitutional Convention.

CauseofLiberty.blogspot.com – for information on Daniel Carroll.

ColonialHall.com – for information about the signers of the Declaration of Independence.

DSDI1776.com – for information on many Founders.

FamousAmericans.net – for information on many Founders.

FindaGrave.com – for burial information, vital statistics and obituaries.

FirstLadies.org – for information on Abigail Adams.

Newspapers.com – Hundreds of newspaper articles were accessed—too numerous to mention here.

NPS.gov – for information on various park sites.

TeachingAmericanHistory.com – for information on Charles Pinckney and George Wythe.

TheHistoryJunkie.com – for information on multiple Founders.

USHistory.org – for information on multiple Founders.

Wikipedia.com – for general historical information.

Index

INDEX

INDEX

INDEX

Call to Action:

The authors, Joe Farrell, Joe Farley, and Lawrence Knorr, have traveled throughout the eastern United States to visit all of the graves of the Founders of the U.S.A. The biographies and grave information of more than two hundred of these most important contributors to our nation's founding can be found in their four-book series Grave of Our Founders. This book, *Pennsylvania Patriots*, is the first regional book pulled from the chapters of the series, focusing on the Commonwealth of Pennsylvania. Along the way, during their thousands of miles on the road, visiting urban, suburban, and remote rural settings, the team has sadly found about one-third of the graves to be in disrepair or otherwise suffering from neglect. We call upon you and others like you who recognize the essential contributions these people made to American history and, therefore, world history. If you find one of these patriot graves in disrepair near your hometown, rally to the cause. Organize a group to address the concerns and properly honor our founders so future generations may do so.

The Graves of Our Founders team has a website dedicated to conveying information about the condition of these patriot graves. Please follow us at www.AdoptaPatriot.com.

CPSIA information can be obtained
at www.ICGtesting.com
Printed in the USA
LVHW052126140221
679286LV00005B/1102